Introduction

You may be someone with low-grade non-Hodgkin lymphoma. Perhaps someone close to you has this kind of lymphoma. You are not alone: each year in the UK more than 17,000 people are diagnosed with lymphoma (including CLL, described on pages 97–102), making it the fifth most common cancer.

Low-grade non-Hodgkin lymphoma is not just one illness. There are several different types but they are all slow growing. In some ways, having low-grade lymphoma is not at all what you might expect of 'having cancer'. Most people with low-grade lymphoma enjoy a good quality of life for long periods of time, often needing very little or no treatment for months or even years. But there are challenges in living with low-grade lymphoma and this booklet aims to help you learn to deal with these. It will explain what low-grade lymphomas are, how they behave and what happens when they do need treatment.

Lymphomas are complex, so sometimes we and your doctors and nurses will have to use medical words. To help you understand these, we will explain what they mean when we use them or in the glossary. Words marked like **this** can be found in the glossary.

People often want to know more about their own kind of low-grade lymphoma. Part 5 of this booklet gives more details about the most common types of low-grade lymphoma. It tells you how each type differs from other lymphomas.

As we have covered many different treatments and many low-grade lymphomas, we don't recommend that you read the whole of this booklet from cover to cover. In Parts 4 and 5, we suggest that you read only the sections about your own type of low-grade lymphoma or about treatments that you are going to have. Looking at sections about other lymphomas could be confusing or even misleading.

People with lymphoma and those close to them often tell us it feels like they're on an emotional rollercoaster. It can be hard dealing with practical problems that can happen during your treatment too.

 You will find more about the sorts of feelings people often have and some ways you might help yourself or your loved one in Part 6 (see page 117). You will find tips for coping with side effects in the appendix at the end of this booklet.

This booklet is about low-grade non-Hodgkin lymphoma. We have more information about other types of lymphoma and on living with your lymphoma.

If you would like to talk to someone about lymphoma or have any questions, please ring our confidential Freephone helpline (0808 808 5555), email us on information@lymphomas.org.uk or contact us via Live Chat on our website (www.lymphomas.org.uk). Here you will also find several active forums where you can post messages and share your experiences.

Acknowledgements

This booklet is the sixth edition of a booklet first published in 2006. We would like to thank our Medical Advisory Panel, Lymphoma Nurse Specialists and other expert advisers for their ongoing help in developing our publications. In particular we would like to thank these experts for their help in the 2014 revision of this booklet:

Dr Eve Gallop-Evans, Consultant Clinical Oncologist, Velindre Cancer Centre, Cardiff

Dr Graham Collins, Consultant Haematologist, Oxford University Hospitals NHS Trust

Tracy Mitchell-Floyd, Lymphoma Clinical Nurse Specialist, Oxford University Hospitals NHS Trust

Thank you also to all those people affected by lymphoma who have helped us by making suggestions on what to include or by reviewing the revised text.

Finally, thank you to all those who continue to offer support to others affected by lymphoma through our website and forums – some of their words of support and encouragement have been used as quotes in this booklet.

Disclaimer

We make every effort to make sure that the information we give you is accurate but it should not be relied upon to reflect the current state of medical research, which is constantly changing. If you are concerned about your health, you should consult your doctor. The Lymphoma Association cannot accept liability for any loss or damage resulting from any inaccuracy in this information or third-party information such as information on websites which we link to.

The information in this booklet can be made available in large print.

Contents

3 Treatment overview for low-grade non-Hodgkin lymphoma

4 More about treatments for low-grade non-Hodgkin lymphoma 49

Understanding low-grade non-Hodgkin lymphoma

The lymphatic system

What is lymphoma?

How and why do lymphomas develop?

Symptoms of lymphoma

How are lymphomas classified?

1 The lymphatic system

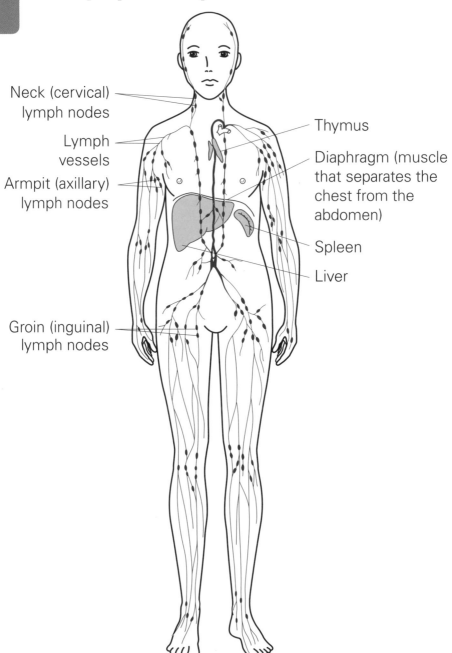

Neck (cervical) lymph nodes

Lymph vessels

Armpit (axillary) lymph nodes

Thymus

Diaphragm (muscle that separates the chest from the abdomen)

Spleen

Liver

Groin (inguinal) lymph nodes

1

Our lymphatic system is made up of a complex network of tubes (known as lymph vessels), glands (known as **lymph nodes**) and other organs such as the **spleen**. We have lymph nodes and lymph vessels throughout our bodies. Some groups of lymph nodes may be easily felt, for example under the arms, in the neck and in the groin. Others are deeper inside us and can only be seen on scans.

The lymphatic system is part of the body's natural defence against infection – the **immune system**. The lymph nodes are an important part of this defence, acting as a sieve in the lymphatic system. They are a home to large numbers of **lymphocytes** (a type of **white blood cell** that helps our bodies to fight infection).

 If you would like to know more about the lymphatic and immune systems please ring our helpline (0808 808 5555), email us on information@lymphomas.org.uk or see our website (www.lymphomas.org.uk).

What is lymphoma?

Lymphomas are cancers of the lymphatic system. They occur when some of the lymphocytes become cancerous.

Lymphoma is not just one illness. There are many different kinds but they all start with a cancerous lymphocyte.

Lymphoma was first described in the 19th century by Dr Thomas Hodgkin. One kind of lymphoma known as Hodgkin lymphoma (or Hodgkin's disease) is named after him; all other kinds are known as non-Hodgkin lymphoma.

1

Non-Hodgkin lymphomas are much more common than Hodgkin lymphoma. Each year, over 15,000 people in the UK are diagnosed with a type of non-Hodgkin lymphoma (including chronic lymphocytic leukaemia). These lymphomas can occur at any age, but they are more common in people aged 50 and over.

'To say the diagnosis was a shock is an understatement. I was always very active and loved keeping on the move.'

How and why do lymphomas develop?

Our lymphocytes are always dividing to make new lymphocytes. When fighting an infection, lots of new lymphocytes are made very quickly. Only those that target the infection we have at the time are useful to the immune system. Any lymphocytes that do not target that infection will die, meaning it is only the useful lymphocytes that survive. All of this usually happens in a carefully controlled way.

Lymphomas can occur when there is a breakdown in the control of this system. Instead of dying in the normal way, untargeted 'rogue' lymphocytes start to divide in an uncontrolled way. The rogue lymphocytes collect together to form a lump, most commonly in a **lymph node**. This is a lymphoma.

The rogue lymphocytes can also collect in other parts of the body to form lymphoma. These areas, such as the **spleen**, liver, gut, skin and **bone marrow**, are known as **extranodal** sites.

For most lymphomas, the exact trigger that causes the changes and makes the lymphocytes become cancerous is still unknown. Despite this, it is important that you know:

- You have not done anything to yourself to cause lymphoma.
- You did not inherit it from your parents.
- You didn't catch it and you can't pass it on to others.

1

Some people are more at risk of lymphoma because they have other illnesses, especially if these affect their immune system. Some kinds of lymphoma are known to be linked with certain **viruses** or **bacteria**. We have highlighted this in the detailed information about those lymphomas.

Symptoms of lymphoma

Many people with low-grade lymphoma notice very few **symptoms**; some have none at all.

'I had no lumps, no symptoms and the cancer was found totally by accident. I still can't believe I have this inside me, as other than fatigue I am well.'

People with lymphoma can, however, have many different symptoms. Some of these are common to many cancers. For instance, the lymphoma cells take up energy and nutrients that are needed by healthy cells, so people often feel very tired.

The most common symptom of lymphoma is:

- a painless lump or swelling, often in the neck, armpit or groin. This is a swollen **lymph node**.

1

Often people with low-grade lymphoma will have swollen lymph nodes in more than one place. Sometimes these lymph node swellings can even seem to come and go.

Other possible symptoms include:

- weight loss for no obvious reason
- drenching sweats, especially at night
- fevers and flu-like symptoms that don't go away

these are known as **B symptoms**

- loss of appetite
- itching all over
- trouble shaking off infections.

Sometimes people can have lymphoma in other parts of the body, including the stomach, bowel and skin. In this case there may not be any lymph nodes or other lumps to feel. Symptoms can vary, depending on where the lymphoma is. For example, lymphoma can cause:

- abdominal or chest pain
- diarrhoea or change in bowel habit
- jaundice
- an ongoing cough or shortness of breath.

There is no one symptom that is unique to lymphoma, but a mixture of these symptoms is typical.

With low-grade lymphomas, sometimes the symptoms will get better or at least stay the same – even if the lymphoma isn't treated. Over time, however, more symptoms will usually develop and the symptoms will tend to get worse. For some people with low-grade lymphoma, this will not happen for many months or even years.

How are lymphomas classified?

1

There are different kinds of lymphocyte, any of which can become cancerous, so there are also many different types of lymphoma.

'I had never even heard of my diagnosis, let alone knowing that there were so many types and different categories.'

Lymphomas are classified (or divided and sorted) in three broad ways:
- Hodgkin lymphoma or non-Hodgkin lymphoma
- T-cell or B-cell non-Hodgkin lymphoma
- high-grade or low-grade non-Hodgkin lymphoma.

Doctors will classify your lymphoma by looking in detail at the cells. They will want to know what the cells look like under the microscope and what **proteins** they have on their surface. Other specialised tests may also be needed, for example tests to find out about any changes affecting the genes within the lymphoma cells.

The classification of your lymphoma is very important. It will give your doctor vital information about your illness and tell them:
- what kind of lymphocyte has become cancerous
- whether the lymphoma is growing quickly or slowly
- how the lymphoma may behave, for example what parts of your body are likely to be affected
- what kind of treatment you will need.

What does T-cell or B-cell non-Hodgkin lymphoma mean?

Lymphomas happen when a **lymphocyte** divides in an uncontrolled way because it has become cancerous. Lymphocytes are either B lymphocytes (often known as **B cells**) or T lymphocytes (**T cells**).

B cells and T cells mature in different parts of the body: B cells in the **bone marrow**; T cells in the thymus (a gland found in the chest; see page 10). Both cells help protect the body from infection and illness but do so in slightly different ways.

A cancerous B cell can turn into a B-cell lymphoma; a cancerous T cell can turn into a T-cell lymphoma. Low-grade lymphomas are almost always B-cell lymphomas (apart from some rare T-cell lymphomas that affect only the skin, which are known as 'cutaneous T-cell lymphomas').

What does 'low grade' mean?

Non-Hodgkin lymphomas are described as either high grade or low grade:

- 'High grade' means the cells are dividing quickly, so the lymphoma is a fast-growing or 'aggressive' type.
- 'Low grade' means the cells are dividing more slowly, so the lymphoma is a slow-growing type.

You may also hear low-grade lymphomas called 'indolent' lymphomas.

Low-grade lymphomas are usually made up of mainly small cells that divide slowly. The speed at which the cells divide controls how fast the lymphoma grows.

1

This will vary from person to person, even if they have the same type of lymphoma. It can also vary over time, meaning sometimes the lymphoma will be more active and faster growing than at other times.

What is meant by 'transformation'?

Sometimes a low-grade lymphoma can start to grow much more quickly. The lymphoma cells change to become larger (faster-growing) cells. If enough of the cells change and grow faster, the lymphoma becomes more like a high-grade lymphoma. This is known as **transformation**.

Sometimes only one area of a lymphoma will change (transform). This can mean one lump is high grade and the rest are still low grade. If any part of your lymphoma has transformed, you will need to have the same treatment that someone with high-grade lymphoma would have.

 If you would like to know about high-grade non-Hodgkin lymphoma and its treatment please call our helpline (0808 808 5555) or see our website (www.lymphomas.org.uk).

1

Key facts

Lymphomas are cancers of the lymphatic system. There are many different types of lymphoma.

Lymphomas develop when some of the lymphocytes become cancerous and start to grow out of control.

The causes of lymphoma are not fully understood.

Lymphomas may cause very few symptoms. The commonest symptom is a painless lump – a swollen lymph node. Other symptoms include weight loss, night sweats and tiredness.

Lymphomas are either Hodgkin lymphoma (Hodgkin's disease) or non-Hodgkin lymphoma. Non-Hodgkin lymphomas can be fast growing (high grade) or slow growing (low grade).

They may develop from B cells or T cells. B-cell lymphomas are more common than T-cell lymphomas.

Diagnosis and staging

How is lymphoma diagnosed?

Other tests you may need

What does the 'stage' mean?

How is lymphoma diagnosed?

The word **diagnosis** simply means finding out what is wrong. In most cases, it is not possible for a GP to confirm whether or not you have lymphoma. Your GP will send you to a doctor at a hospital for further tests. These will almost certainly include a **biopsy** and/or a **bone marrow** test.

In a few people, lymphoma will be found in a tissue removed for another reason, without anyone having suspected it was there.

Having a biopsy
For most people, a biopsy is the only way to tell whether or not a lump is lymphoma. It is a test that removes some of your cells so they can be looked at under a microscope. These cells can come from a swollen **lymph node** or from a lump in another part of your body.

Sometimes a low-grade lymphoma will be found in a biopsy of the bone marrow first (see page 23).

The method used to take your biopsy will depend on where your swollen lymph nodes or lumps are and what the doctors in your hospital prefer to do. **Note:** if you are taking medicines to thin your blood, you may be asked to stop these for a while before having your biopsy.

If you have a node that can easily be felt, a surgeon may remove either all or part of it (an **excision biopsy**). Sometimes a **radiologist** may take a small sample of the lymph node or lump (a **core biopsy**) instead.

If your swollen nodes are all deep inside you, a surgeon may need to remove either part or all of a node using laparoscopic (keyhole) surgery. Instead of this, a radiologist may be able to take a core biopsy. They will usually scan you at the same time to make sure they test the right area.

2

If you have an excision biopsy or laparoscopic surgery, you will need to have a general **anaesthetic**. Most people need to stay in hospital at least for a night after a laparoscopic biopsy. This may also be the case after an excision biopsy. For a core biopsy, you will probably only need a local anaesthetic and may be able to go home the same day.

The biopsy will be looked at under the microscope by an expert lymphoma **pathologist**.

There are many different types of lymphoma and making an accurate diagnosis is vital. If needed, the pathologist will arrange further tests on the biopsy to decide exactly what type of lymphoma you have. This is why it is important that the biopsy taken is big enough for all the tests to be done – if there isn't enough tissue sometimes a second biopsy is needed.

Other tests you may need

Your doctors may want you to have other tests as well as your biopsy. This section is about some of the common tests for lymphoma, but don't worry if you don't have all of these tests. Your doctor will arrange the ones that are best for you – sometimes only a few of them are needed to find out about your lymphoma.

2

For most of these tests you can be an outpatient, meaning you won't have to stay in hospital overnight. It may take a couple of weeks for all the results to be available.

It is normal for you to feel anxious while waiting for these tests and the results. It's very important though that your doctors have all the information they need about your lymphoma. This will help them choose the most suitable treatment for you.

Also, because your lymphoma is slow growing, it's not likely to change much during this time. This means the wait should not affect how successful your treatment will be.

'It is normal to feel frustrated whilst waiting for a full diagnosis. In fact I found this stage the worst part.'

Blood tests

You will have blood samples taken when you are first diagnosed and regularly afterwards. Blood tests are done for many reasons:

- to check for **anaemia** or other low blood cell counts
- to check that your kidneys and your liver are working well
- to give your doctors an idea of how your lymphoma may behave
- to look for infections such as hepatitis or **HIV**, which may also need treatment or could flare up with lymphoma treatments.

Bone marrow biopsy

The **bone marrow** is the spongy, jelly-like middle part of some of our bones and it is where blood cells are made.

Your doctors may want you to have a bone marrow biopsy to see if there are any lymphoma cells there. This is quite common in people with low-grade lymphoma. Your doctor will let you know if you need this test when telling you about your diagnosis. They may also call it a bone marrow 'aspirate' or bone marrow 'trephine'.

If you are taking medicines to thin your blood, you may be asked to stop these beforehand. The whole test takes around 15–20 minutes.

A sample of bone marrow is usually taken from your hip bone using a special biopsy needle. The skin and area over the bone is first numbed with a local **anaesthetic**. Despite this, taking the sample can sometimes be painful, although it is usually done very quickly. Sedatives or Entonox® (gas and air) can help some people, but you'll need to talk to your doctor beforehand as they aren't always advisable.

X-rays and scans

X-rays

X-rays can be used to look at various parts of your body. For example, a chest X-ray may be used to see if there are any swollen **lymph nodes** in your chest. X-rays are painless and shouldn't take longer than a few minutes.

2

CT scans

Computed tomography (CT) scans use a series of X-rays to form pictures of your body in cross-section, like 'slices' through your body.

The test involves lying on a padded table that moves your body into a doughnut-shaped camera. The space is quite open so you shouldn't feel claustrophobic (hemmed in). As the table moves, the camera takes pictures of the different layers of your body.

You might be given a special dye (a 'contrast agent') to drink or as an injection before the scan. This makes it easier to see some of your internal organs. The scan is painless and usually takes only a few minutes.

You will be asked to lie quite still while the pictures are being taken. You might also be asked to hold your breath for up to 20 seconds at some stage during the scan.

Talk to the staff in the department if you are worried about any aspect of having your CT scan done.

MRI scans

Magnetic resonance imaging (MRI) scans are similar to CT scans, except they make pictures of you using strong magnets and radio waves instead of X-rays. The pictures are slightly different and are particularly good for looking at certain tissues such as the brain.

You'll be asked to lie on a padded table that moves you into a cylinder (tube). The cylinder measures radio waves as they pass through your body. The test is painless but can take up to an hour. If you would find it uncomfortable to lie still for this long, you might need to take painkillers beforehand, but ask your doctor about this.

The scanner can be very noisy and, as you are in a small space, you may feel claustrophobic (hemmed in). You'll be asked to take off any metal jewellery and clothing with metal parts that could be magnetic. The staff will also ask if you have any metal implants, such as a hip replacement or a pacemaker.

Let the staff in the department know if you are worried about any aspect of having an MRI scan done.

PET scans

Positron-emission tomography (PET) scans can help doctors work out which cells in your body are cancerous and which are not. They use a radioactive sugar to show up the most active cells in the body, and lymphoma cells are usually very active.

A CT scan is often done at the same time and this is called a 'PET/CT scan'. It can give a clearer picture of exactly which areas are affected by the lymphoma. This can be important when your doctors decide which treatment you should have, particularly if you may have localised lymphoma.

Having the scan is painless and the whole process usually takes 2–3 hours. It is very like having a CT scan but advice about what to do before and after your scan may be different – it is important to follow any advice you are given. If you have diabetes, you'll be given instructions to help you keep your sugar levels stable.

If you have any concerns about having a PET scan, talk to the staff in the department – they understand that this scan is something new for most people.

 To find out more about tests for lymphoma please ring our helpline (0808 808 5555) or see our website (www.lymphomas.org.uk).

What does the 'stage' mean?

Once all the test results are ready, your doctor will be able to tell which parts of your body are affected by your lymphoma. This is called the 'stage' of your lymphoma. It will be important in planning your treatment. These are the different stages used for most low-grade lymphomas.

Stage I	One group of **lymph nodes** affected
Stage II	Two or more groups of lymph nodes affected on one side of the **diaphragm**
Stage III	Lymph nodes affected on both sides of the **diaphragm**
Stage IV	Lymphoma can be found either in the **bone marrow** or in organs that are not part of the lymphatic system

Letters can be added to the stage too. 'B' would mean you have B symptoms (weight loss, night sweats or fevers); 'A' would mean you have none of these.

The letter 'E' would mean you have **extranodal** lymphoma (lymphoma outside your lymphatic system).

Most people with low-grade lymphoma will have lymphoma that is at stage III or IV by the time they are diagnosed. This is because the lymphoma grows slowly and you may have had it for a long time before you developed any symptoms.

2

Although there are four lymphoma stages, in terms of treatment doctors think about low-grade lymphomas in two different groups:
- early-stage (localised) lymphoma, or
- advanced-stage lymphoma.

Advanced-stage lymphoma may sound alarming but there are good treatments available for lymphoma at all disease stages.

The stages are usually grouped as follows:
- Stage I lymphomas are early-stage lymphomas.
- Stage II lymphomas may be treated as early-stage or advanced-stage lymphoma – those causing symptoms, with large lumps or affecting groups of lymph nodes that are not next to each other are more likely to be treated as advanced stage.
- Stage III and IV lymphomas are advanced-stage lymphomas.

If you are not sure whether your lymphoma is early stage or advanced stage, we suggest you check with your doctor – the treatments for these stages may be quite different.

Key facts

2

Lymphoma is normally diagnosed by a biopsy. This means that cells are removed to be looked at under the microscope.

Usually a swollen lymph node is sampled – either by removing all or part of it, or by taking a smaller 'core' biopsy. A number of special tests will be done on the sample to decide exactly what type of lymphoma you have.

You may need to have other tests, such as a bone marrow biopsy and scans. Your doctor will arrange the ones that are best for you.

The results allow your doctors to work out the stage of your lymphoma. This information is important in planning the right treatment for you.

Treatment overview for low-grade non-Hodgkin lymphoma

3

About your treatment

Treatments for low-grade non-Hodgkin lymphoma

What happens during treatment?

What happens when I am not on active treatment?

What happens if low-grade lymphoma comes back?

About your treatment

Aims of treatment

The aim of your treatment will depend on whether you have early-stage or advanced-stage lymphoma. It may also depend on the exact type of lymphoma you have and on your age and general fitness.

When talking about the aims of your treatment, your doctors may use these words:

- **Remission** – the lymphoma has been controlled by the treatment; this may be either:
  - a complete remission (no lymphoma can be seen on the scans), or
  - a partial remission (the lymphoma has shrunk by at least a half).
- **Relapse** – the lymphoma has come back after being in remission or has flared up after a quiet period.
- **Cure** – the lymphoma has been treated to the point where it has gone and will not come back in the future.

Early-stage low-grade lymphoma

Fewer than 1 in 5 people with low-grade lymphoma will have early-stage lymphoma (lymphoma that is affecting only one or two groups of **lymph nodes** or areas in just one part of the body). For these people, there is a chance that their lymphoma can be cured by their treatment.

Although doctors may be aiming for a cure, they often prefer to talk about remission rather than cure. This is because they cannot say for sure whether your lymphoma will relapse. With low-grade lymphoma, a relapse can happen many years later, but the longer you stay in remission, the less likely you are to relapse.

Advanced-stage low-grade lymphoma

This term may sound alarming but it just means that several groups of lymph nodes or different areas of the body are affected by the lymphoma. Most people with low-grade lymphoma have advanced-stage lymphoma. Most of them will live for many years with their lymphoma and enjoy a good quality of life.

3

Advanced-stage low-grade lymphoma behaves more like a **chronic** (long-term) illness. It usually goes into remission – either complete or partial – but then often relapses and needs further treatment. This pattern of flaring up and then settling down again after treatment is sometimes known as a 'relapsing and remitting' course.

Doctors treating someone with this type and stage of lymphoma will be aiming to keep the lymphoma under control. This means they want the lymphoma to cause no, or very few, symptoms for as much time as possible. Because low-grade lymphoma is hard to get rid of permanently, they will also think carefully about the possible side effects of any treatment.

Planning your treatment

Once your doctors have the results of all the tests, they will be able to plan your treatment. Your doctors are part of a team known as a multidisciplinary team (MDT). The team includes other experts who look after people with lymphoma too. They will meet to check all your test results and think about the most suitable treatment for you.

Your treatment will depend on the type and stage of your lymphoma and what problems, if any, it is causing.

Other points the team will think about include:
- your thoughts on treatment and what is important to you
- your general health and usual level of fitness
- any other illnesses you have and how these affect you
- your blood test results.

3

Finishing the tests and planning your treatment can take a couple of weeks. This might seem a long time, but the information being collected is very important. Your doctor needs to know as much as possible about you and your lymphoma before choosing the best treatment.

You will probably feel worried when you are waiting to find out more or waiting to start your treatment – this is only natural. You may find it helps to talk about this to someone, maybe a specialist nurse or your GP.

Where will I be treated?

People with lymphoma can be treated at local hospitals or at larger hospitals that have a specialist cancer centre. Sometimes the treatment is shared between the two.

Your GP, or the doctor who finds out that you have lymphoma, will send you to the nearest hospital that has a doctor who is an expert in treating lymphoma. You may see either a **haematologist** (a doctor who specialises in treating blood problems) or an **oncologist** (a doctor who specialises in treating cancer).

If you have a rare type of lymphoma you may be referred to a specialist cancer centre. The doctors there are likely to have seen more people with your type of lymphoma. They may also be running a clinical trial (see page 35) that you could enter if you wanted. The doctor at your local hospital might still treat you nearer home with guidance from the cancer centre.

Your doctor will not mind if you want to ask questions about your hospital and how they plan to give you the care you need.

3

Other questions that might be important to ask are:
- Will your doctor meet regularly with other lymphoma experts at an MDT meeting?
- Does the hospital have a clinical nurse specialist or other specialist cancer nurses?
- Does the hospital take part in clinical trials and is there one that would be suitable for you?
- What other experts are there to help if you need them? For example, will you be able to see a dietitian or a counsellor if you need to?

Will my doctor help me to decide about having treatment?

For some people with low-grade lymphoma, doctors will suggest that treatment is not needed straightaway. This is known as **watch and wait** (you will find more about this approach on pages 50–53). Your doctor is likely to suggest this if you do not have any symptoms and it is safe to delay any treatment for a while.

For other people who are having problems because of their lymphoma, one or more treatments will be recommended.

Either way it is important you understand and are happy with what is going to happen.

3

For people who are normally quite fit and likely to cope well with treatment, deciding to go ahead with treatment may be simple.

For other people, the decision may be harder. Perhaps the treatment is less likely to put their lymphoma into **remission**. They may be more at risk of side effects with the treatment. Sometimes, it can be hard to weigh up all the benefits and the risks, especially if there is more than one possible treatment – for example, a strong treatment and another that is more gentle.

Your doctor will help you decide what treatment to have. Talk to your doctor, clinical nurse specialist, and family and friends who are supporting you if you are finding it hard to make a decision. Make sure you understand what is being recommended for you and any choices you have. Ask as many questions as you need to help you with your decision.

Many people find it helps to take a relative or friend along to their hospital appointments. Your companion may remember things that are said that you don't recall. They may remind you of other questions that they know you wanted to ask. Your doctor won't mind. In fact most doctors encourage their patients to bring someone along. You may want to take a notebook and pen with you too in case you want to write anything down.

 We produce a booklet with suggested questions you may like to ask about lymphoma, the tests you will need and the treatments you might be offered. Please ring our helpline (0808 808 5555) or see our website (www.lymphomas.org.uk).

Research and clinical trials

You may be asked if you would like to take part in a clinical trial. These are scientific studies that often test medical treatments.

Some trials are designed to test new treatments that haven't yet been tried in a particular type of lymphoma. Others are looking to improve on current treatments, perhaps by changing one of the drugs or adding in something new. Clinical trials are very important in improving the future treatment for people with lymphoma.

Each clinical trial is usually just for people with one type of lymphoma, or sometimes a few similar types. For some trials, only people in a certain age group will be allowed to take part. Having other illnesses may also stop some people going into a trial, so they are not suitable for everyone.

Not all hospitals take part in clinical trials and some trials will be run in only a few centres. It is important to ask about clinical trials that may be suitable for you, especially if you have a rare type of lymphoma. Your doctor may be able to refer you to another centre if you would like treatment in a clinical trial.

Clinical trials are entirely voluntary. You do not have to take part in a trial if you do not wish to. You can always opt to have the standard treatment if you prefer. It is important you understand fully what is involved before you agree to take part in a trial, especially if you would have to travel some way to take part – you should be given written information. If you change your mind later on, you are free to withdraw from the trial at any time.

If you do take part in a trial you will be more carefully watched or may have more tests. Apart from this, however, you may not get any direct benefit – no one can say which treatment is better until the trial is finished. The one certain fact is that you will be helping other people to have the best possible treatment for lymphoma in the future.

3

 We produce a booklet on clinical trials. Please ring our helpline (0808 808 5555) or see our website (www.lymphomas.org.uk) if you would like a copy.

Treatments for low-grade non-Hodgkin lymphoma

Early-stage lymphoma
The standard treatment for most people who have early-stage lymphoma is radiotherapy to the area affected. This works well if the lymphoma is affecting only one area of the body and is not too large. A PET/CT scan may be done to make sure there is no lymphoma elsewhere in the body.

Surgery is not usually the best treatment when there is lymphoma in any **lymph nodes**. This is because some cancerous cells are often left behind so the lymphoma is very likely to come back.

Some people with stage II lymphoma are treated in the same way as people with more advanced lymphoma. This might be the best choice if your lymphoma has formed a large lump or is in groups of lymph nodes that are not next to each other. It might also be best if you are getting symptoms or if your blood tests suggest any other organs could be affected.

The treatments for advanced-stage lymphoma are also used if early-stage lymphoma **relapses**.

Advanced-stage lymphoma

If you have advanced-stage low-grade lymphoma, there are a number of different treatments that your doctor might suggest. These vary from having a period of active monitoring, known as **watch and wait** to having **intravenous** chemotherapy, such as R-CVP or R-CHOP.

⟶ You will find more about the different kinds of treatment in Part 4. In Part 5 you will be able to see what treatments are commonly used to treat your type of low-grade lymphoma.

You may be surprised or worried if your doctors suggest that you do not need to start treatment at once. Do not think this is because they do not want to treat you or that your lymphoma cannot be treated. Research shows that watching and waiting for as long as possible really is the best choice for people with low-grade lymphoma who are well. Your doctors will give you treatment as soon as your lymphoma starts to give you symptoms, which may be now or may be in the future.

When it is needed, most people will have treatment with some form of chemotherapy, along with an **antibody**. For some types of low-grade lymphoma, this treatment is followed by **maintenance treatment**. The aim of this is to keep the lymphoma in remission or under control for as long as possible. It means having antibody treatment alone once every 2–3 months. It can, however, continue for up to another 2 years so it needs to be thought about carefully.

For some people, if only one area of their lymphoma is causing them problems, radiotherapy may be used. This involves giving a low dose of radiation to just the one area, for instance to shrink a painful lump and ease symptoms. Any other swollen glands can then be watched again until they start to cause problems.

Sometimes low-grade lymphoma can **transform** into a faster-growing type of lymphoma – more like a high-grade lymphoma. If this happens, it will need to be treated in the same way as a high-grade lymphoma would be. Often this treatment will get rid of the high-grade part of the lymphoma, but it will leave behind a small amount of low-grade lymphoma. These slow-growing lymphoma cells can start to grow again in the future, leading to a **relapse** of the low-grade lymphoma.

There are lots of different possible treatments for advanced-stage low-grade lymphoma. The exact treatment that is chosen for you will depend on:

- the type of lymphoma you have: some lymphomas respond better to certain kinds of treatment than others; some treatments are not suitable for all lymphomas
- side effects and safety: some treatments are likely to cause more side effects and can be harder to tolerate, especially if you have other health problems – your doctor will want to make sure that your treatment does not do more harm than good

- the need for a quick response: if you have severe symptoms or your lymphoma is causing problems with a major organ, it will need to be treated quickly – some therapies work faster than others
- convenience: for instance, how often you need to visit the hospital, whether you are likely to need to be admitted, the total time your treatment will take and what you would prefer.

3

Lymphoma treatments in older people

More than half of people diagnosed with non-Hodgkin lymphoma are over 65.

Treatments for non-Hodgkin lymphoma sometimes have to be adjusted in older people to make them safer. Doctors will not decide on your treatment based on your age, but they will think very carefully about any other health problems you have. Such problems often become more common as people get older.

Your doctors will need to be sure that the treatment they are recommending is safe for you. For example, if your heart isn't working well, they may avoid giving you certain drugs that could make it worse.

Sometimes people who are older can be more troubled by side effects and may take longer to recover from them. Your doctors may adjust your treatment to lower the chances of you getting side effects.

If you are older or less fit, your treatment will be carefully planned just for you. It will depend in particular on how well your heart, lungs and kidneys are working.

3

Your doctors may arrange for you to have special tests, such as an echocardiogram (often just called an 'echo') or lung function tests, before you start any treatment. Talk to your team about what is happening and why.

Your doctors will want to give you as much treatment for your lymphoma as they feel is safe. They will balance this against the risks of making you more ill with the treatment and any possible complications. This might mean that your treatment has to be slightly different from the treatments we describe for younger people.

Don't be afraid to ask your doctor about your treatment and why they feel it is the best treatment for you.

It may be that some of the new targeted therapies will make treatment for older people easier and better. Clinical trials are now even looking at the possibility of treating some types of low-grade lymphoma without chemotherapy. Your doctor will be able to tell you whether there are any suitable clinical trials that you could enter.

⟶ You will find more information about targeted therapies on pages 76–79.

What happens during treatment?

Day-to-day life
It is hard to predict exactly how you will feel during your treatment and how it will affect your day-to-day life. If you have had lots of symptoms from your lymphoma, you may feel much better once you start treatment. Some people have few side effects from their treatment

and are able to carry on almost as normal; others will have side effects that mean they need to make changes, at least for a while.

'The key was to learn from my body. If it wanted to do very little then that's what we did and conserving energy was the aim at all times.'

3

→ More information on possible side effects is given on pages 57–65 for chemotherapy, pages 75–76 for antibody therapy and pages 81–86 for radiotherapy.

Working

If you normally work, you should let your employers know what is happening – most will be sympathetic and flexible, and you have a number of rights in law.

At the very least, you are going to need to take time off work for hospital appointments. In practice, most people take a lot more time off or need to work fewer hours or change the work they are doing.

Your hospital team will be able to offer you more advice depending on your treatment and the sort of work you do. For some people the risk of infection may mean that work is not advisable while they are having chemotherapy.

'I have managed to work quite a lot through the chemo, though sometimes at home not the office.'

If you are unable to work, you will probably be entitled to sick pay. This will not be the case if you are self-employed. In this case you will need to try to plan how you will manage your work and finances.

If you are unemployed, you should advise your local Department for Work and Pensions (DWP) office of your illness as your benefit payments will probably change.

Ask at your hospital as they may have a specialist benefits/welfare adviser you could see.

 Please ring our helpline if you would like to talk about work, finance or benefits (0808 808 5555). Macmillan Cancer Support produces information about work and cancer too – see page 134 for their contact details.

Hobbies and socialising

It is important that, while being treated for lymphoma, you allow yourself time to do things you enjoy. When you feel well enough, you should try to continue as much as possible with your hobbies – do check with your hospital team if your usual hobbies are adventurous, very active, or in any way dangerous.

You will also probably feel better if you can maintain your social life as far as possible. Seeing a few friends, getting out or having a change of scenery can help to make you feel more 'normal'. Do be aware though that there may be times when you should avoid crowds because of the risk of infection – your hospital team will be able to give you more advice about this.

'Since being diagnosed I appreciate life more, even small things like hearing the birds sing and seeing the sun shine. I take a lot more out of life and try to enjoy every minute of it.'

Holidays and special events

For most people having treatment for low-grade lymphoma (other than **maintenance treatment**), a holiday, especially outside of the UK, may not be the best idea. It may, however, be possible to make small changes to your planned treatment so that you can be away from home for a while. Tell your hospital team in plenty of time if you have any special events or plans, so that they can offer you the best advice.

Even if you are thinking about a holiday when you have finished treatment, do talk about this with your team. You might need to think about where you travel to, your accommodation and whether you will need any vaccinations. Finding travel insurance at a reasonable price can also be a problem, so it is important to think ahead.

 For more information about all aspects of travel and holidays please ring our helpline (0808 808 5555) or see our website (www.lymphomas.org.uk).

Sex and contraception

There is no reason why you should not have sex during treatment if you feel like it, but you should continue to use contraceptives during treatment. This is because treatments may damage sperm or eggs and could be harmful to a developing baby. Also, if a woman is pregnant, it can make it harder to treat the lymphoma.

Advice varies but doctors will often give this advice to people having chemotherapy:

- Women with lymphoma should not become pregnant during their treatment and for some time afterwards (some doctors recommend 2 years).
  Note: oral contraceptive tablets may not work as well while you are on treatment, so talk to your doctor or nurse about this.
- Men with lymphoma should avoid making their partner pregnant while they are having chemotherapy and for at least 3 months afterwards (some doctors recommend longer).

If this is an issue for you, do talk about it with your hospital team. They will then be able to give you specific advice as your circumstances could be different.

➡ You will find more information about the effects of treatment on fertility on page 64.

Traces of chemotherapy can stay in the body for up to 5 days after treatment. Condoms should be used during this time and you should avoid oral sex and open-mouth kissing where saliva is exchanged, as body fluids may contain traces of chemotherapy.

 For more information about sexuality and lymphoma please ring our helpline (0808 808 5555) or see our website (www.lymphomas.org.uk).

What happens when I am not on active treatment?

People with low-grade lymphoma typically spend much of the time not having active treatment. This may be because they are on **watch and wait** or because they have finished a course of treatment.

3

Usually, people who are not on active treatment will have regular follow-up appointments in the hospital clinic – typically once every 3–6 months.

If you are worried about your health at any time, you don't have to wait for your next appointment. You should get in touch with your GP or hospital team to talk about your concerns. They might arrange an early clinic appointment for you.

Even if you are not on active treatment, it is important that you can ask questions and get advice when you need it, so make sure you have the contact details for your hospital team.

You will also have a chance to talk about anything that might be on your mind when you go for your hospital appointments. It can help to write things down when you think of them and take a list of questions with you.

Normally at follow-up appointments you will be asked about how you are feeling and will have a brief physical examination. You may also have some blood tests.

Unless your doctors think your lymphoma could be relapsing, you probably won't have scans or X-rays.

This is because, if you are well, your doctor won't change the way they want to treat you just because of a scan result. Also, repeated scans that give you lots of small doses of radiation over many months or years could actually do you harm.

3

When you do have a problem, your doctor will then arrange to investigate it in the best way.

What happens if low-grade lymphoma comes back?

Unless you had early-stage lymphoma, it is most likely that your low-grade lymphoma will **relapse** at some time. You and your doctors will then need to decide on the next course of treatment. Over time, most people with low-grade lymphoma have several courses of treatment.

Where possible your doctors will probably suggest using different drugs for each course of treatment. The average time between treatments is 2–3 years, but the gap will probably shorten with repeated courses. If you are fit enough, further treatments may be stronger than your first treatment and might include a stem cell transplant – these should give you a longer time in **remission**.

Having a good quality of life is, however, also very important. Your doctors will think carefully about your likely quality of life when they plan your treatment. They will also be keen to know what your views are on having further treatment.

There are lots of treatments available that work very well for low-grade lymphoma that has relapsed. When choosing your treatment, your doctors will think about what treatment you had before and how you found it, as well as how long ago you had the treatment.

Make sure you understand what the doctors are recommending for you and why. Don't be afraid to ask questions and talk to your team about your choices.

3

The good news is that, even though most low-grade lymphomas still relapse, people now live longer than they did a few years ago. New treatments, including a number of targeted therapies, are also becoming available or are being tested in clinical trials. The outlook for people with low-grade lymphoma, even after it has come back, is therefore getting better all the time.

 If you would like to talk about your lymphoma or its treatment please ring our helpline (0808 808 5555), email us on information@lymphomas.org.uk or contact us via Live Chat on our website (www.lymphomas.org.uk).

Key facts

Your treatment will depend on the type and stage of your lymphoma as well as on your age and health.

Early-stage low-grade lymphomas may be cured, but these are not common.

Advanced-stage low-grade lymphomas behave like a chronic illness: they will need treatment from time to time but your quality of life between treatments should be quite good.

No one can say for sure how you will feel and what you will be able to do while you are having treatment. Ask your team about the side effects you are likely to have and find out about any choices you have.

It is likely you will have periods of months or even years when you are not on active treatment. During these times you will still have check-ups regularly. If you are worried about anything, you don't have to wait until your next appointment. Call your hospital team or your GP to talk about your concerns.

There are lots of treatments available if low-grade lymphoma comes back. New treatments mean the outlook for people with low-grade lymphoma is getting better all the time.

3

More about treatments for low-grade non-Hodgkin lymphoma

4

Watch and wait

Chemotherapy

Antibody therapy

Other targeted therapies

Radiotherapy

Stem cell transplants

Watch and wait

Many people who have stage III or IV low-grade lymphoma – and some with stage II low-grade lymphoma – do not need treatment at once. You may not need to start treatment yet if:

- you feel well and have no 'B' symptoms (see page 14)
- you have small **lymph nodes** that are not causing problems or growing quickly
- your doctors are happy with your blood test results
- none of your other organs are affected.

If you feel reasonably well, you may have no active treatment until your symptoms become harder to live with. Delaying active treatment like this means you will avoid having side effects. It also saves the treatments until you really need them.

This is known as the 'watch-and-wait' approach – also sometimes called 'active monitoring'. You will be watched (or actively monitored) at clinic appointments, usually every few months. Your doctors will check on your lymphoma and will want to know how you are feeling. If all is well, you will wait until your lymphoma starts to cause you problems before you start having active treatment. These problems might include:

- feeling much more tired
- having pain or discomfort from swollen lymph nodes
- not being able to carry on with your normal day-to-day life.

Clinical trials have shown that people who don't have chemotherapy straightaway do just as well as people who do. People can stay on watch and wait without

4

needing active treatment for anything from a few months to many years.

Doctors usually recommend watch and wait as the standard approach for people with advanced-stage low-grade lymphoma who feel well. Some people may instead be offered treatment with the **antibody** rituximab. Giving rituximab on its own has been compared with watch and wait in clinical trials. These show that having rituximab for 2 years can delay the need for chemotherapy but this may not be any better in the long term. It is also not yet clear if chemotherapy given with rituximab after this will work as well.

4

'Watch and wait is something hard to get your head around, but now I am further along I can really appreciate this option as it buys you time with very few symptoms.'

Living with watch and wait
It can be hard to have a cancer and not be having active treatment. Some people find it hard to accept that it seems that nothing is being done about their lymphoma.

People often misunderstand the reasons for watch and wait. It does not mean that you are too old or that your lymphoma is too advanced to treat. It's just that the evidence shows that you will be better off saving treatment until your lymphoma is causing more of a problem.

 If you would like to talk about watch and wait, please ring our helpline (0808 808 5555) or contact us via Live Chat on our website (www.lymphomas.org.uk).

It is important though that you go to your clinic appointments and tell your doctors if anything changes. Your doctors may want to see you sooner if you notice new symptoms or that your lymph nodes are growing more quickly or starting to grow in new places. If this happens, it could be a sign that you need to start treatment.

4

The symptoms to look out for are the typical symptoms of low-grade lymphoma. These include:
- loss of appetite and weight loss
- fevers for no obvious reason
- drenching sweats, especially at night
- feeling more tired, even when you haven't done much
- itching all over, but with no skin problems or rash.

'It scares me to think that the lymphoma is growing away inside me and we are doing nothing about it.'

These symptoms can often occur for other reasons, such as getting an infection with a **virus**. Therefore if you notice any of these symptoms, you shouldn't panic. Unless your symptoms are really dramatic or are getting steadily worse after a few days, you can afford to wait a week or so to see if you get better again. Even if the symptoms are due to your lymphoma becoming more active, there is rarely any rush to start treatment – low-grade lymphoma usually grows very slowly.

It is also quite common for swollen glands to grow a little, then shrink again without any treatment. This is another reason not to rush into treatment but to wait until your doctors decide it is clearly needed.

When you are not on treatment, it is important you try to keep your life as normal as possible and do the things you most enjoy. You might also want to use this time to get yourself as fit as possible before you need treatment. But sometimes it can be hard to cope with not being on treatment.

'Currently I'm on watch and wait and at the moment I don't feel any different. So my way of dealing with it is to just take one day at a time and deal with whatever comes my way when it arrives. I don't think about the future – I just live in the here and now.'

4

→ You will find more about coping with your feelings while on watch and wait on pages 119–120 and on changes you might want to make to your life on pages 121–122.

Chemotherapy

What is chemotherapy?
The word 'chemotherapy' means treatment with drugs. Drugs for cancer are called 'cytotoxic' because they kill cells: 'cyto' means cell and 'toxic' means poisonous.

Chemotherapy works by stopping the cancer cells dividing. Different chemotherapy drugs do this in slightly different ways. Chemotherapy for lymphoma often involves giving more than one kind of drug. This increases the chances of killing as many cancer cells as possible.

Chemotherapy works particularly well on cells that are dividing quickly and less well on cells that are dormant (resting). To target as many cells as possible, chemotherapy is generally given as repeated blocks of treatment (often called **cycles**). With each treatment cycle, more cells are destroyed and the lymphoma gradually shrinks.

Each cycle also has a rest period when no chemotherapy is given. This is because normal cells, such as those in the **bone marrow** and the lining of the mouth and bowel, are also damaged by chemotherapy. The rest period allows the healthy normal cells time to recover. You may still have other medicines to take during this time, for example to protect you from side effects.

How is chemotherapy given?

Chemotherapy for low-grade lymphoma is very often given as an outpatient treatment. This means you will not normally need to stay in hospital overnight. If your treatment is given as tablets only, you will probably collect these after a clinic visit and then go home. If part of your treatment is **intravenous**, you will be treated in a day treatment unit and go home later the same day.

You will probably have a number of cycles of chemotherapy (often six to eight), each taking a few weeks. The exact timetable for your treatment will depend on what kind of chemotherapy you are having. Your hospital team will give you specific information about your treatment and what to expect.

Whatever treatment you are having, you may need to stay in hospital if you get severe side effects, for instance very low blood counts or an infection.

→ You will find more about the most common side effects of chemotherapy on pages 57–65.

Chemotherapy for low-grade lymphoma can be given in a number of different ways:
- intravenously, meaning through a thin tube into a vein (the most common way)
- orally, meaning by mouth in tablet or capsule form
- subcutaneously, meaning by an injection given just under the skin (used for only a few drugs).

4

Intravenous chemotherapy
Intravenous drugs for low-grade lymphoma are typically given through a cannula (a small plastic tube that goes into a vein, usually on the back of your hand or in your lower arm). Once the drugs have been given, the cannula is taken out. A new one is put in each time.

Some intravenous drugs are given as a 'bolus'. The drug is 'pushed' through the cannula using a syringe, usually over a few minutes. Intravenous chemotherapy can sometimes make your arm sting. Tell the nurse if you feel any discomfort.

Other intravenous drugs are given as a drip (an infusion). The drug is put into a bag of fluid, which then drips through the cannula over many minutes (or sometimes hours). A pump may be used to make sure the drip goes in over the correct time. The drip and the pump are often hung on a stand with wheels, so you can walk around.

A few people with low-grade lymphoma – for example those having high-dose chemotherapy – will need to have chemotherapy that is spread over many hours or even days. They will need to be an inpatient for this treatment. Often this kind of chemotherapy is given through a more permanent intravenous tube (or 'line') instead of through a cannula. This makes it easier and safer to give the drugs that are needed. Sometimes lines are also used for people having problems with cannulas for outpatient chemotherapy.

There are two kinds of line: a PICC line (peripherally inserted central catheter) and a tunnelled central line. A **PICC line** usually goes in through a vein in the arm near the bend of the elbow. It's held in place by tape or a dressing. A **tunnelled central line** is usually positioned on the upper chest. Part of the line runs in a tunnel under the skin, which reduces the risk of infection. You may hear these called Hickman® or Groshong® lines.

Such lines can often stay in place for all the cycles of treatment. They must be kept covered and need a bit of extra care when people are out of hospital – this is quite simple and many people learn to do it for themselves. There is a risk they can become infected though, so it's important to know the signs to watch for (see page 59).

Oral chemotherapy
Often people need to take oral chemotherapy as part of their **regimen**. Some people with low-grade lymphoma will have chemotherapy that can all be taken orally.

You will collect your tablets or capsules from either the day treatment unit or from the hospital pharmacy. The person giving you the medicines should tell you what to take and when. This information will also be on the boxes or bottles containing your treatment.

Chemotherapy tablets or capsules should not be handled by anyone other than the person taking them. If you are a carer helping someone to take their chemotherapy, you should wear disposable gloves when handling any tablets or capsules.

The side effects of oral chemotherapy are often easier to cope with than those of intravenous chemotherapy. This means oral chemotherapy may be a good choice for anyone who is not fit enough to cope with stronger intravenous chemotherapy.

4

Subcutaneous chemotherapy
At present, only a few chemotherapy drugs are given subcutaneously, but there may be more in the future.

A nurse will inject the drug through a tiny needle into the layer of fat just under your skin – usually on your tummy, upper arm or thigh. The injection is quick and easy to give. It may cause some brief stinging or aching but is not usually too painful.

Side effects of chemotherapy
It is not possible to say what side effects you will have from your treatment. Everybody will notice slightly different side effects, even if they are having the same treatment as someone else.

The side effects of chemotherapy will depend on what drugs you are having. Your hospital team will give you information about what to expect.

Generally, the stronger your chemotherapy, the more side effects you are likely to have.

If you would like to talk about the side effects of chemotherapy please ring our helpline (0808 808 5555) or contact us via Live Chat on our website (www.lymphomas.org.uk).

It is important to let your hospital team know about your side effects and whether any of them change. There are usually things that can be done to help.

Over the next few pages we describe some of the more common side effects of chemotherapy. There are side effects that could affect you during or soon after your treatment, and also side effects that could affect you later on, perhaps months or even years after your treatment.

→ You will find tips for coping with some of the common side effects of treatments for lymphoma in the appendix on pages 138–144.

Risk of infection and low blood counts
The most important side effect to know about is damage to the **bone marrow**. The job of your bone marrow is to make your body's blood cells. These include your white blood cells that help to fight infection. The most important **white blood cell** is called a **neutrophil**.

You may hear a low white cell count referred to as **neutropenia**, meaning the number of neutrophils is low. This can happen with any chemotherapy. It is more common after the stronger chemotherapy **regimens** sometimes used for low-grade lymphoma. It means you will be more at risk of infection. The white cell count tends to be lowest about 7–10 days after each dose of chemotherapy, but it can stay low for some time.

If you are neutropenic (have neutropenia), your chances of getting an infection are higher. If you develop an infection, it can be serious and sometimes it can even be life-threatening. You should call your hospital **at once** if you develop signs of an infection. These can include:

- fever
- temperature of 38°C or above (though your temperature might not be raised if you are taking steroid tablets; see pages 66–67)
- chills, shivering or sweating
- mouth sores and ulcers
- cough or sore throat
- redness or swelling of the skin, especially around your line if you have one or where you've had a cannula
- diarrhoea or abdominal pain
- burning sensation when passing urine
- feeling generally unwell or disorientated.

4

An infection in someone who has very low neutrophils needs to be treated urgently. This will usually mean going into hospital as an emergency for **intravenous** antibiotics. You should make sure you keep the contact numbers for your hospital handy at all times.

If you have to ring the hospital because you are not feeling well, do tell the person you speak to that you are having chemotherapy. That way they can make sure you get the best advice and get treatment quickly if you need it. If you are on a clinical trial, make sure you tell them about this too.

➡ You will find tips on how to lower your risk of infection if you are neutropenic on pages 138–139.

Many people still feel well even when their blood count is low. If your white cell count is too low when your next cycle of treatment is due, your doctors may delay this until your blood count has had a chance to recover. You may need to have other drugs to help boost your blood count after further cycles of chemotherapy. These are called **growth factors** or **G-CSF** (see page 67).

4

Sometimes other blood cells can be affected by chemotherapy. Your **red blood cells** carry oxygen. A lack of these is called **anaemia**, which can make you feel tired or short of breath.

This is quite common because low-grade lymphoma can sometimes cause anaemia even before chemotherapy is given. Other people may develop anaemia after they have received several cycles of chemotherapy. Some people may need blood transfusions to ease their symptoms of anaemia.

Platelets help to stop you bleeding. A lack of platelets is called **thrombocytopenia**, which can make you more likely to bruise easily or bleed. People who are bleeding or have very low platelet counts are sometimes given a transfusion of platelets.

You will have regular blood tests taken to check your blood counts during your treatment.

Feeling sick
Some chemotherapy drugs may make you feel sick (or nauseous) after treatment. You might vomit too. You will be given anti-sickness drugs to help. These are called 'antiemetics'.

Tell your doctor or nurse if you are feeling sick. If you are taking anti-sickness drugs that aren't working, tell one of your hospital team. There are lots of different anti-sickness drugs and sometimes a change of drug is needed.

Sore mouth
Chemotherapy drugs may give you a sore mouth. This is because the chemotherapy damages the cells of the lining of your mouth. This is called 'mucositis' and can be painful. It can also make you more prone to mouth ulcers and infections. Your hospital team will be able to advise you about mouthwashes and painkillers that can help.

4

Change in taste and other dietary problems
It is quite common for people being treated with chemotherapy to have other problems with eating such as loss of appetite or finding that foods taste different or unpleasant.

Fatigue
Fatigue is one of the most common symptoms for people with lymphoma.

Cancer-related fatigue is quite different from normal tiredness. It can mean that you find it hard to concentrate or make decisions. It may make you short-tempered. You might sometimes feel too tired to do even simple things, like watching television. Fatigue can be hard to describe, and you may find that other people don't really understand it.

You may find that you are more fatigued as you come to the end of your course of treatment. It may be some months after treatment before your fatigue goes away.

There is good evidence that taking some regular gentle exercise can help people feel better more quickly.

 For more information about fatigue please ring our helpline (0808 808 5555) or see our website (www.lymphomas.org.uk).

Hair loss

Some chemotherapy drugs used to treat low-grade lymphoma cause hair loss. This means that you may lose some or all of your hair.

If it is going to happen, thinning of your hair will typically begin within a couple of weeks of starting treatment. It can fall out quite suddenly, which can be very distressing. Ask your team about wig facilities that are available on the NHS in your area or for advice on other headwear.

Your hair will usually start to grow back within a month or two of your treatment finishing. Sometimes it may seem different, perhaps curlier or a slightly different colour. It will probably take 6–12 months for it to return to its normal thickness.

You will find some tips for dealing with hair loss on pages 142–143.

Peripheral neuropathy

Some chemotherapy drugs cause damage to the nerves that carry information about touch, temperature and pain. The drugs can also damage other nerves, including the nerves involved in muscle movement. This nerve damage is called 'peripheral neuropathy'.

Peripheral neuropathy is usually due to certain groups of drugs. One drug often used in low-grade lymphoma that can cause neuropathy is vincristine (part of the CVP and CHOP regimens).

→ You will find more information about the CVP and CHOP regimens on pages 68–69.

Neuropathy commonly affects the nerves in your hands and feet, but you might feel it in other places too. It can sometimes affect the nerves to the internal organs, which is known as 'autonomic neuropathy'.

4

It can cause:
- pins and needles
- pain
- numbness
- clumsiness
- problems with balance
- increased sensitivity to heat
- constipation
- temporary impotence.

Symptoms of neuropathy usually develop soon after you start treatment, but not everyone will get them. If you have any of these symptoms, you should tell your doctors or nurses **before** you have your next dose of chemotherapy. They may want to make a change to your treatment to prevent these problems getting worse.

For most people, symptoms of peripheral neuropathy will be temporary, but some people can have long-term or permanent nerve damage.

Effects on fertility

Some treatments for lymphoma may reduce your fertility. Many people are able to have children after treatment without any problem, but certain chemotherapy drugs – especially the high-dose chemotherapy used in stem cell transplants – can make this less likely. Women closer to the age of normal menopause are more likely to have problems with fertility.

4

Your doctor will not be able to say for certain how your fertility might be affected, but they should talk about this with you before you start treatment.

Men may wish to think about sperm storage before they start treatment. Being ill with lymphoma can reduce your sperm count even before you start treatment. However, developments in fertility treatment mean that sperm storage is still worthwhile for many men who may want to have children in the future.

The choices for women are more limited, partly because fertility treatments in women take more time. This could mean any lymphoma treatment is delayed, which may not be good for your health in the long term.

If this is an issue for you, you should talk to your team about seeing a specialist to find out more about what choices you have. Embryo storage may be possible for some women but it does take time. Egg storage and ovarian tissue freezing are newer techniques and are not offered at all hospitals. Different hospitals will also have different policies about the funding of these treatments on the NHS.

Women may find that their periods become irregular or stop altogether during treatment. Afterwards their periods may return to normal but, for some women, the irregularity continues when treatment has finished. Some women, even those who are still fertile straight after treatment, may go through an **early menopause**.

Heart problems

Some drugs, especially doxorubicin (one of the drugs in CHOP), can cause damage to the heart, with problems sometimes developing many years later. You may have special tests such as an echocardiogram (often just called an 'echo') to see how well your heart is working before you start treatment.

Certain drugs may be avoided if your heart function is not good or if you have had heart trouble in the past. Even if your heart is normal, your doctors will be careful not to prescribe more than the safe maximum dose.

Blood problems

Some chemotherapy treatments can lead to a small increase in the risk of developing other blood problems in the future. These problems are very rare but can include myelodysplastic syndrome (MDS) and acute leukaemia.

MDS is an illness where the **bone marrow** no longer makes enough healthy blood cells. It can result in a low **blood count**, most often causing **anaemia** that may need to be treated with blood transfusions.

 Please ring our helpline if you would like to talk about the long-term side effects (late effects) of treatment (0808 808 5555).

Other treatments sometimes given with chemotherapy

Steroids

Steroids are drugs that mimic hormones made naturally by the body. The steroids used in lymphoma treatment help to kill the lymphoma cells. They also reduce nausea and help you to feel better. Steroids are usually given as tablets, often in the form of prednisolone. Some regimens for lymphoplasmacytic lymphoma use **intravenous** dexamethasone instead.

Steroids can have many different side effects, including:

- weight gain – this is partly due to an increase in appetite and may be a good thing if you have been losing weight
- problems sleeping – you should usually try to take your steroids early in the day, if possible before lunchtime
- mood changes – you may feel more restless and irritable; some people find they have most problems on the days just after they have finished taking their steroids
- raised blood sugar – extra care may be needed to monitor your sugar levels if you have diabetes or a tendency towards it
- fluid retention, causing ankle swelling or puffiness of the hands and face
- infections – for example, you may be more likely to develop thrush (caused by candida infection) or cold sores (caused by a virus)
- muscle aches or weakness – people sometimes find it hard to raise their arms, stand up from a chair or climb stairs.

The side effects will depend on the dose used and whether the steroids are given for a short or long time. Always tell your hospital team about any symptoms you have that might be side effects. There are often things that can be done to help. The side effects will improve once you stop taking the steroids.

 For more information about steroids please ring our helpline (0808 808 5555) or see our website (www.lymphomas.org.uk).

Growth factors

Growth factors are copies of hormones that occur naturally in our body. They can help to keep the levels of your **white blood cells** up when you are having chemotherapy.

The growth factor most commonly used is called **G-CSF**. It triggers the **bone marrow** to make more stem cells, which can then become white blood cells.

G-CSF is given as an injection into the fatty tissue under your skin (a **subcutaneous** injection). Most people learn to give the injections themselves or a relative may be taught how to give them. It is sometimes also possible for a nurse to give G-CSF at a GP surgery or even at home, if needed.

G-CSF can cause side effects such as: flu-like symptoms; bone pain, especially in the lower back and pelvis; and headaches. If you feel unwell during your growth factor treatment, you should get in touch with your hospital straightaway.

4

CVP and CHOP chemotherapy

One of the most commonly used chemotherapy **regimens** for low-grade lymphoma is known as CVP. Another similar regimen is known as CHOP. Both involve giving several drugs together.

CVP is made up of three drugs:
- two **intravenous** drugs, **c**yclophosphamide and **v**incristine; and
- oral **p**rednisolone tablets.

4

You usually don't need to stay in hospital to have this treatment – it is normally given in a day treatment unit. The intravenous drugs are given on the first day of each **cycle** and you will be given the prednisolone tablets to take at home for the first 5 days of each cycle. This is followed by a rest period – you may still have other drugs to help prevent side effects during this time. Cycles usually last 3 weeks and a full course of treatment is usually six to eight cycles.

CHOP is the same as CVP but with one extra drug: **h**ydroxydaunorubicin (often known as doxorubicin), also given intravenously on the first day of each cycle. The letter 'V' is replaced by an 'O', using the brand name for vincristine (**O**ncovin®) instead.

Adding the drug hydroxydaunorubicin means that CHOP has more side effects than CVP. The benefits are that it works more quickly and it also works against high-grade lymphoma. For some people, this might be important if their doctors are concerned about possible **transformation** of the low-grade lymphoma to a faster-growing type.

For many people with low-grade lymphoma the **antibody** rituximab (MabThera®) is added to the CVP or CHOP regimen. The treatment is then known as **R-CVP** or **R-CHOP**.

Rituximab therapy is described in more detail on pages 72–76.

Other chemotherapy regimens

Bendamustine
Another drug that is used for low-grade lymphomas is bendamustine (Levact®). It is given as a short intravenous infusion (drip), usually on the first 2 days of each cycle. This is repeated every 3–4 weeks for up to six cycles.

People who have received bendamustine are advised that any future blood products they receive should be irradiated (see page 71).

Bendamustine is at present licensed in the UK for use on its own in people with certain low-grade lymphomas who have **relapsed** quickly after treatment with rituximab and as the first treatment for some people with chronic lymphocytic leukaemia/small lymphocytic lymphoma.

In clinical trials bendamustine has often been given together with a dose of rituximab on the first day (**R-bendamustine**). These trials suggest that R-bendamustine works at least as well as R-CVP and R-CHOP in advanced-stage low-grade lymphoma. It also causes fewer side effects.

4

Bendamustine is at present approved by NICE (National Institute for Health and Care Excellence) for use only in certain people with chronic lymphocytic leukaemia/small lymphocytic lymphoma. At the time of writing, the Cancer Drugs Fund in England will pay for it to be used in some people with other lymphomas too. Therefore its use has become more common in recent years.

Fludarabine

4

A different kind of drug called a purine analogue is sometimes used in other chemotherapy **regimens**. The commonest drug of this type used in lymphoma is called fludarabine (Fludara®).

Fludarabine can be given intravenously or in tablet form. It is usually given daily for 3–5 days, followed by a rest period. A cycle lasts 4 weeks and typically up to six cycles are given. People who have received fludarabine are advised that any future blood products they receive should be irradiated (see page 71).

Fludarabine is often used together with other drugs, such as cyclophosphamide and rituximab.

The regimen **FCR** is made up of:
- **f**ludarabine and **c**yclophosphamide – given either as tablets for 5 days or intravenously for 3 days every month
- the antibody **r**ituximab – given intravenously at the start of each **cycle**.

Within the NHS at present, FCR is approved as a treatment only for people with chronic lymphocytic leukaemia/small lymphocytic lymphoma.

Fludarabine stops the body's normal **T cells** working properly. This increases the risks of certain infections due to **viruses**, so you are more likely to develop cold sores or shingles, for example.

It also increases the risk of pneumonia (a chest infection) caused by a fungus known as *Pneumocystis jiroveci* (known in the past as *Pneumocystis carinii* pneumonia or PCP). Your doctors will give you an antibiotic to lower the risk of this infection during and after your fludarabine treatment.

4

Note on irradiated blood: People who have been treated with fludarabine or bendamustine are advised that any blood products they receive in future should be irradiated. This means that before being transfused the blood is treated with X-rays to kill off all the unwanted **white blood cells** in the donated blood. This prevents a rare complication of blood transfusion known as 'transfusion-associated graft-versus-host disease' (TA-GvHD) from developing.

Your doctors will give you more information about TA-GvHD and a card to carry in your wallet or purse. They will tell your hospital's blood bank in case you need blood during your treatment. You should continue to have irradiated blood for the rest of your life.

More information is available from the National Blood Service at: http://hospital.blood.co.uk/library/pdf/ Irradiated_Blood_13_12_05.pdf (accessed August 2014).

Chlorambucil

Another tablet form of chemotherapy often used for older people with low-grade lymphoma is a drug called chlorambucil (Leukeran®). It is taken every day for 10–14 days. People are often given steroid tablets (prednisolone) to take on the same days. They then have 2 weeks off chemotherapy but may still take other medicines to protect against side effects. This forms a cycle of treatment, which is usually repeated each month.

4

A full course of treatment usually lasts about 6 months, but can sometimes be longer. For a few people, chlorambucil is given at a low dose every day instead.

Clinical trials are now suggesting that chlorambucil may work better if an antibody, such as rituximab or a newer drug (obinutuzumab or ofatumumab), is also given as part of the treatment.

Antibody therapy

What is antibody therapy?

Antibodies are **proteins** in our blood that fight infection. They are made naturally by our bodies when we have an infection. They stick to proteins called 'antigens' on the surface of **bacteria** or **viruses** and tell our bodies to get rid of them.

Lymphoma cells have proteins on their surface too and these can be used as a target for treatment. Antibodies can be made in a laboratory to recognise these antigens. When the man-made antibody matches with and sticks to a lymphoma cell, it marks the cell out to be killed by the body's **immune system**.

Antibody therapy (sometimes called 'immunotherapy') is different from chemotherapy and radiotherapy because it targets cancer cells more directly. This means it does not have the same side effects as chemotherapy or radiotherapy.

The antibody most often used for low-grade lymphoma is called **rituximab** (MabThera®). Other, newer antibodies are also starting to be used to treat some people with low-grade lymphoma or are being tested in clinical trials. These include **ofatumumab** (Arzerra®) and **obinutuzumab** (known in its early trials as GA101). All of these antibodies target a protein called CD20.

4

Because CD20 is found only on **B cells**, rituximab, ofatumumab and obinutuzumab are normally used to treat only B-cell lymphomas.

Another antibody treatment called **alemtuzumab** (MabCampath®), which you may hear called 'Campath', may also be used to treat a few people with chronic lymphocytic leukaemia/small lymphocytic lymphoma. This antibody targets a protein called CD52, which is also found on B cells. If your doctor is thinking about this treatment for you, they will talk to you more about what is involved.

Other new antibodies that will target different proteins found on lymphoma cells are being developed and tested in clinical trials. In other trials antibodies that are linked to chemotherapy drugs are also being tested. The antibody targets the lymphoma cells and delivers the chemotherapy, which kills the lymphoma cells but causes less damage to other healthy cells.

How is antibody therapy given?

Rituximab

Rituximab for low-grade lymphoma may be given either together with chemotherapy (usually at the start of each **cycle** of treatment) or on its own. For some types of low-grade lymphoma, it may be used as **maintenance treatment** following a course of chemotherapy. This aims to reduce the chances of the lymphoma coming back quickly. In this case, it is given every 2–3 months for up to 2 years.

Rituximab is usually given to you as an outpatient, so you don't normally have to stay in hospital. The first dose of rituximab is given as a drip (an infusion) into a vein. It must be given slowly to help prevent side effects. This may take a few hours.

After the first dose, infusions may be given more quickly (over about an hour) if people have not had a bad reaction before.

It is also now possible for certain people with lymphoma to have these later doses of rituximab as an injection into the layer of fat just under the skin (a **subcutaneous** injection). This means each dose can be given in about 5 minutes. Your doctor will be able to tell you whether this is suitable for you.

 For more information about rituximab please ring our helpline (0808 808 5555) or see our website (www.lymphomas.org.uk).

Ofatumumab

Ofatumumab has been used in trials both on its own and together with chemotherapy. It is given as an **intravenous** drip (an infusion) but very slowly. The first dose will contain a smaller amount of the drug. It is usually given as an outpatient therapy. On its own, ofatumumab is usually given once a week for 8 weeks then monthly for another four doses.

Obinutuzumab

Obinutuzumab has been used in trials, usually together with chemotherapy (such as chlorambucil). It is given as an intravenous drip (an infusion) but very slowly and the first dose is split over 2 days. There are usually extra doses given in the first month of treatment. It is usually given as an outpatient therapy.

4

Side effects of antibody therapy

Most side effects of antibodies that are given intravenously occur while the infusion is being given (known as 'infusion-related side effects') rather than later on. They are more common with the first infusion and include shivers, fevers and other flu-like symptoms. When given subcutaneously, the skin where the injection was given may become red, swollen and painful. You will be given other drugs such as paracetamol and antihistamine to help reduce the chances of these problems.

Rarely, people have more serious side effects caused by an allergic reaction. If this happens, you may need to stay in hospital for a while as you recover. You may be able to have the infusion more slowly in future or your doctor may decide it is best to avoid this treatment.

Antibodies can also lower the **white blood cell** count, increasing the risk of infection. This is not very common.

← You will find more details about low blood counts on pages 58–60.

A very small number of people receiving rituximab have developed a viral brain infection known as PML (short for 'progressive multifocal leukoencephalopathy'). This is a serious complication but fortunately it is very rare.

Each antibody has slightly different side effects – your doctor will be able to tell you more about any other side effects you might expect.

Other targeted therapies

What are targeted therapies?

Targeted therapies are sometimes also called 'biological therapies'. This is because they use specific biological pathways to target the lymphoma cells.

The main kind of targeted therapy used in lymphoma is antibody therapy (see pages 72–76). There are, however, other targeted therapies available to treat some types of low-grade lymphoma. As doctors learn more from the results of clinical trials, more targeted therapies are starting to be used. Further trials are needed to work out how and when it is best to use these new drugs.

There are different kinds of targeted drugs, which work in different ways. The following are some of the targeted drugs that are now being used or tested in low-grade non-Hodgkin lymphoma.

Radioimmunotherapy

This treatment involves an antibody that is used to deliver a particle of radiation directly to the lymphoma cells. Because it targets the **B cells**, the radiation kills the lymphoma cells but causes less damage to other healthy cells.

The treatment ^{90}Y-ibritumomab tiuxetan (**Zevalin**®, see page 96) is licensed in the UK, but is not widely available within the NHS and can only be given in a few UK hospitals.

Cell signal blockers

We now understand a lot more about the pathways within lymphoma cells that keep them alive or make them divide. Often signals reaching the surface of the cell trigger a series of steps along one or more pathways. Scientists have found that blocking either the signal or a key step in the pathway can make lymphoma cells die.

A number of new drugs have been developed to target these signals and pathways. **Ibrutinib** (see pages 96, 101 and 115) and **idelalisib** (see pages 96, 101 and 115) target two different pathways that both help B cells stay alive and divide. Blocking these pathways makes the cells in many B-cell lymphomas die.

Proteasome inhibitors

There are many **proteins** that help to control what happens in cells and how they divide. Proteasome inhibitors, such as **bortezomib** (Velcade®, see page 114), upset the balance of these proteins. This seems to be particularly harmful to certain lymphoma cells, causing the cells to die.

4

Immunomodulators

Doctors think that these drugs work by changing (or 'modulating') how the **immune system** works.

Lenalidomide (Revlimid®, see page 96) may do this in a number of ways. These include blocking some of the signals between immune system cells, blocking some of the signals inside lymphoma cells, and stopping new blood vessels growing in or around the lymphoma. The lymphoma cells are 'starved' of the support they need, so the lymphoma stops growing.

How are targeted therapies given?

This varies for different drugs but many of them are given by mouth (orally).

Zevalin is a one-off treatment but requires two visits to the hospital, usually about a week apart. At the first visit a dose of rituximab is given. At the second visit, more rituximab is given, and this is followed by the Zevalin.

You can go home after each visit. You will need to take extra care though for the first few days after having Zevalin – your doctor will be able to tell you more.

Bortezomib was in the past given into a vein but it is now also available for injection just under the skin (a **subcutaneous** injection).

Lenalidomide, ibrutinib and idelalisib, like many of the newer targeted therapies, are taken as tablets. Usually these tablets are taken on many or all of the days in each **cycle**.

Side effects of targeted therapies

The side effects vary for different drugs. In general, targeted therapies often cause fewer side effects than standard chemotherapy.

They can make people feel more tired, especially if they are taking lenalidomide. Other side effects can include nausea or bowel upset. Hair loss is not generally a problem. Bortezomib can also cause peripheral neuropathy (see pages 62–63).

Most targeted therapies can affect the **bone marrow**, so there is still a risk of infection and bleeding. This is usually less of a problem than with most chemotherapy **regimens**.

4

If your treatment includes a targeted therapy, your doctor will give you more information about what side effects to expect.

Radiotherapy

What is radiotherapy?

Radiotherapy uses high-energy X-rays, similar to those used to take an X-ray picture, but given in much higher doses. The X-rays are directed to precise areas. They can kill off cancer cells in this area by stopping them dividing.

Radiotherapy is used for some people with low-grade lymphoma. Lymphoma cells are very sensitive to radiotherapy but the treatment can only be given to small areas. It is therefore used to treat early-stage (localised) lymphoma. It may also be used to treat certain small areas in more advanced-stage lymphoma.

How is radiotherapy given?

A course of radiotherapy is usually given as a series of sessions known as 'fractions'. These are usually given daily, Monday to Friday, and you can go home after each treatment. The number of fractions will vary but treatment is often spread over a period of 2–3 weeks.

Your radiotherapy care will be led by a clinical oncologist (or **radiotherapist**), who will talk with you about your treatment beforehand.

 If you would like to talk about your radiotherapy treatment please ring our helpline (0808 808 5555).

Treatment planning

This may involve more than one visit to the department before treatment starts. You will need to have a special scan to produce a precise map of the area to be treated. This is then used to plan exactly where your radiotherapy will target.

The **radiographers** will need to make sure you are in exactly the same place on the treatment couch every time you have treatment, so they will mark dots on your skin to help. They will use a type of marker pen or will ask you if they can make some more permanent tiny ink marks on your skin. These will look like small freckles and are known as a 'radiotherapy tattoo'.

If you are having radiotherapy to the head or neck area, a shell will be made, usually from a plastic mesh. This will keep your head still and in the correct position. It also means that you will not need any marks on your skin.

Having the treatment

During your treatment, the radiographers will position you carefully on the couch and ask you to stay very still. You will be in the treatment room for 10–20 minutes, but much of this time is spent getting you in exactly the right place. The actual treatment takes only a few minutes and you will not feel anything.

This kind of radiotherapy does not make you radioactive. There will be no risk to those close to you.

4

Side effects of radiotherapy

The side effects of radiotherapy will depend on what part of your body is being treated and the amount of radiotherapy given. You will be given information about what to expect and how to take care of yourself.

You may find that you have no side effects to start with but that they gradually become more obvious as you go through your course of treatment. They are often at their worst shortly after the treatment has finished, then start to improve.

Most radiotherapy side effects are short term and settle down. Some may be long term or permanent. Your doctors should talk about this with you before you start treatment. In general, radiotherapy doses for low-grade lymphoma are quite low so the side effects are not usually too bad.

 If you would like to talk about the side effects of treatment ring our helpline (0808 808 5555).

It is important to let your hospital team know about your side effects. There are usually things that can be done to help. You may also be seen in a review clinic during your course of treatment.

➡ You will find some tips for coping with the side effects of lymphoma treatments in the appendix on pages 138–144.

Over the next few pages we will describe some of the more common side effects of radiotherapy.

Fatigue

Fatigue (extreme tiredness) is one of the most common problems for people with lymphoma. Fatigue is also a common side effect of radiotherapy. It may be many weeks or sometimes even a few months after treatment before you recover fully.

⬅ You will find more information about fatigue on pages 61–62.

Sore skin

The skin in the area being treated may become pink, dry and itchy. If you have dark skin it might become darker. Rarely the skin can blister, a bit like sunburn. This is more likely to happen in folds of skin such as under the breast or in the groin. Skin reactions are usually at their worst a few days after the end of treatment and then start to heal.

You will be told how best to care for your skin. You may be asked to be careful when washing and drying the area. You may be given creams to keep the skin moisturised.

Hair loss

If you are having radiotherapy, hair loss or thinning should only occur in the area being treated. This hair loss will usually only be temporary. Your hair should start to grow back a few months after treatment.

Sore mouth and problems swallowing

If you are having radiotherapy to the head, neck or upper chest, you may find that your mouth or throat becomes sore. You may also find that food starts to taste different or metallic.

4

If the area of the radiotherapy includes your salivary glands, your mouth will also become very dry. Your doctors may recommend artificial saliva or drugs to increase the amount of saliva you produce to help with this. It may take several months for this side effect to improve and sometimes it may be permanent.

If you are having radiotherapy to the chest or neck, you may also find that swallowing becomes a problem for a while.

Risk of infection and low blood counts

Radiotherapy may affect your **blood count**, particularly if certain bones are in the area being treated. If the white blood cell count falls (sometimes known as **neutropenia**), this can make you more prone to infections.

You will find some tips on how to lower your risk of infection if you are neutropenic on pages 138–139.

You may also develop **anaemia**. This can make you feel even more tired and can also make you feel short of breath.

Radiotherapy to the **spleen** can make your **platelet** count low. This can make you more likely to bleed or bruise easily, so the count will be checked regularly.

Feeling sick

Sometimes radiotherapy can make you feel sick, in particular if your abdominal area is being treated. If you are feeling sick, tell the **radiographers**. It may help to have anti-sickness drugs (antiemetics) before each treatment starts. If you are taking anti-sickness drugs but they aren't working, tell the radiographers. Sometimes a change in the anti-sickness drug is needed.

Heart disease and stroke

Radiotherapy to an area including the heart will increase your risk of heart disease in the future. This becomes more likely if you have had chemotherapy that also affects the heart. Treatment given to your chest and neck may also increase your risk of stroke in later life. These problems become more common 10 years or more after your treatment.

The risk of this happening to you will depend on the dose of radiotherapy and the exact area treated. You can help to lower the risk by taking good care of yourself, keeping your body at a healthy weight and, if you smoke, giving up. You should also see your doctor for advice about checking for high blood pressure, diabetes and high cholesterol.

Lung problems

Lung fibrosis (scarring) can be a side effect of radiotherapy to the chest. Once it develops, lung fibrosis is usually permanent. If mild it can be seen on X-rays or scans but will not cause you any symptoms. Some people can become short of breath and find they are able to do less exercise than before. The risk of this is lower if you do not smoke.

Thyroid problems

Radiotherapy given to the neck can affect the thyroid gland, reducing the amount of the hormone thyroxine that it makes. A lack of thyroxine in the blood is called 'hypothyroidism'. This may slow your metabolism, so you may feel very tired, gain weight easily or feel the cold more than normal.

4

Hypothyroidism can develop any time after treatment, even many years later. If you are at risk, a blood test to check your thyroid function should be done each year. If this shows your thyroid is becoming underactive, your GP will start you on thyroxine tablets.

There is also an increased risk of developing thyroid cancer many years after radiotherapy to the neck. This is very rare, however, unless you are treated at a young age.

Second cancers

Much of what is known about the higher risks of developing another cancer comes from clinical trials done many years ago in people with Hodgkin lymphoma. At that time people were often treated with high doses of radiotherapy given to large areas of the body. The radiotherapy was also given by machines that were much more basic than today's. People with low-grade lymphoma are now given smaller doses of X-rays in a much more targeted way.

Your risk of developing a second cancer later on depends on the part of your body that is being treated, for example:

- radiotherapy affecting the breast tissue in women, especially if treated at a young age, increases the risk of breast cancer – regular breast screening is recommended from 8 years after the end of your radiotherapy onwards to detect any cancers early; talk to your doctor if this might apply to you
- radiotherapy to the chest increases the risk of lung cancer – stopping smoking is vital to limit this risk.

Your doctor will be able to tell you what your risks are and offer you advice on what to do to reduce these risks.

 If you would like to talk to someone about the long-term effects (late effects) of treatment, please ring our helpline (0808 808 5555) or contact us via Live Chat on our website (www.lymphomas.org.uk).

Stem cell transplants

Some people with low-grade lymphoma may be offered treatment with a stem cell transplant. These might include:

- people with **relapsed** lymphoma
- people who are thought to be at high risk of relapse
- people whose lymphoma has not responded to the standard treatment.

A stem cell transplant may work when standard treatments have not or when they are thought unlikely to be enough. Stem cells are special cells normally found in the **bone marrow** that produce new blood cells. The stem cells used in a transplant may be either **autologous** (your own cells) or **allogeneic** (a donor's cells).

An autologous transplant is a way of safely giving a much higher dose of chemotherapy to your lymphoma – it helps your bone marrow recover more quickly. It should help to keep you in **remission** for longer; for a few people, their lymphoma may never come back.

4

Allogeneic transplants are more complex. The donor's stem cells develop in your bone marrow into a new **immune system** and this helps to kill the lymphoma cells. This is known as a 'graft-versus-lymphoma' effect. It may offer a chance of curing some low-grade lymphomas, which chemotherapy alone cannot do.

Stem cell transplants carry risks as well as benefits, especially if they are allogeneic. This means they are not suitable for everyone. Most people having a transplant need to stay in hospital for some weeks and recovery can take many months. If your doctors are thinking about this form of treatment for you, they will talk to you in detail about it.

 For more information about stem cell transplants please ring our helpline (0808 808 5555) or see our website (www.lymphomas.org.uk).

Key facts

Watch and wait

Watch and wait can be the best approach for some people with low-grade lymphoma who are well and do not need treatment at once.

You will be seen regularly in the clinic but treatment will be kept for when your illness causes you problems, which may be anything from a few months to many years later.

Being on watch and wait does not mean that you are too old or that your lymphoma is too advanced to treat.

If you are someone who finds it hard to cope with not being on treatment, it is important you are honest about your feelings, talk to people and seek help.

Chemotherapy

Chemotherapy means drug treatment, often using several different drugs in each treatment cycle. Treatment usually takes 6 months or more in all, but may sometimes be followed by up to 2 years of maintenance antibody therapy.

Chemotherapy is usually given into a vein (intravenously) and/or as tablets (orally). It will most often be given to you as an outpatient.

There are lots of possible side effects of treatment. Your side effects will depend on what kind of treatment you are having. You should be given information about what side effects to expect.

4

If you develop signs of infection or notice any side effects, you should tell your hospital team at once. There are usually things that can be done to help. An infection in someone who has low neutrophils needs to be treated urgently.

Antibody therapy

Antibody therapies can be given either with or without chemotherapy for some low-grade lymphomas.

They work by sticking to a protein on the lymphoma cell. The antibody marks the lymphoma cell out to be killed by the body's immune system.

4

The antibody most commonly used for non-Hodgkin lymphoma is rituximab (MabThera®).

Rituximab is most often given as an intravenous infusion. For some people, it may now be given as a subcutaneous injection instead. It will normally be given to you as an outpatient.

Flu-like symptoms during the infusion are the most common side effect. You will be given drugs to prevent these.

Other targeted therapies

Targeted therapies are sometimes called 'biological therapies' – they use the biological functions of the body to target the lymphoma cells.

Radioimmunotherapy uses an antibody to target radiotherapy to the lymphoma cells.

Cell signal blockers and immunomodulators aim to stop the lymphoma cells growing.

Many targeted therapies can be given as tablets. Their side effects vary but they are often less of a problem than with chemotherapy or radiotherapy.

Radiotherapy

Radiotherapy may be used to treat early-stage (localised) low-grade lymphoma or an area that is causing a problem in advanced-stage lymphoma.

Your radiotherapy care will be led by a clinical oncologist (or radiotherapist). You will visit the department so that your treatment can be carefully planned beforehand.

Radiotherapy is painless. Each fraction (session) of treatment takes 10–20 minutes in total. It usually continues for 2–3 weeks.

The side effects of radiotherapy will depend on the area being treated as well as the total amount given. They tend to develop towards the end of treatment. You should be given information about what side effects to expect.

If you notice any side effects, tell your hospital team as there are often things that can be done to help.

4

Types of low-grade non-Hodgkin lymphoma

5

Follicular lymphoma

Chronic lymphocytic leukaemia (CLL)/ small lymphocytic lymphoma (SLL)

Marginal zone lymphomas
Gastric MALT lymphoma
Non-gastric MALT lymphoma
Splenic marginal zone lymphoma
Nodal marginal zone lymphoma

Lymphoplasmacytic lymphoma (Waldenström's macroglobulinaemia)

Cutaneous lymphoma

This part of the booklet looks in more detail at the most common types of low-grade non-Hodgkin lymphoma.

You will find a list of the lymphomas in this section in the contents on page 8.

We would suggest that, at least at first, you read only the section on your own type of low-grade lymphoma.

If you are not sure exactly what kind of lymphoma you have, check this with your doctor. It may be confusing or distressing to read about illnesses that are not relevant to you.

We have not been able to give details of every type of low-grade non-hodgkin lymphoma. If you have been told you have a type of lymphoma that you do not see listed in this booklet, you may wish to check with your doctor. They may have used another name for a lymphoma that is included. If not, they might be able to tell you if there is a lymphoma included that is close to yours.

For each lymphoma we are aiming to answer these questions:
- What does the name mean?
- Who typically gets it?
- How might it affect me?
- How might it be treated?

Follicular lymphoma

What does it mean?

The name 'follicular' is used because, when a **lymph node** is looked at under the microscope, the lymphoma cells are found in 'follicles' (or clumps).

Follicular lymphoma is a B-cell lymphoma. In most people with follicular lymphoma, the lymphoma cells have a **protein** called CD20 on their surface. This protein is the target for certain treatments, such as **antibodies**.

Who gets it?

Follicular lymphoma is the most common single type of low-grade lymphoma. Just over 1 in 5 of all people with non-Hodgkin lymphoma will have this type. It is uncommon in people younger than 50 and most people with follicular lymphoma are aged over 65.

5

How will it affect me?

Follicular lymphoma tends to grow slowly in most cases. In the early stages it usually causes very few symptoms. By the time most people develop symptoms, they will have advanced-stage lymphoma. As a result, more than 4 out of every 5 people have stage III or IV lymphoma when they are diagnosed.

The lymphoma cells can build up in the lymph nodes, the **bone marrow**, the **spleen** and the liver. Sometimes they collect in other tissues too. This build-up of lymphoma cells can cause problems, which may include:

- swelling of lymph nodes – the most common symptom – often in more than one place; the nodes will sometimes go up and down in size

- lots of infections because the **immune system** is not working properly
- sweating, tiredness and weight loss
- low blood cell counts, usually due to lymphoma cells collecting in the bone marrow or the spleen. This can cause **anaemia**, which can make you feel short of breath and very tired. The number of **platelets** in your blood might also be reduced. This would make you more likely to bleed or bruise very easily.

Follicular lymphomas are made up of a mixture of small and large cells. The more small cells there are, the slower the lymphoma is likely to grow. If a lymphoma contains mainly small cells, doctors call it grade 1–2. A lymphoma with more large cells is called grade 3a or grade 3b, which means it is likely to grow more quickly. The grade of a lymphoma can change over time.

In the case of grade 3b follicular lymphoma, there are so many large cells that it is likely to grow as fast as some high-grade lymphomas. If your doctors find that you have grade 3b lymphoma, you will probably be offered treatment with a **regimen** that can be used to treat high-grade B-cell lymphoma, such as R-CHOP.

How will it be treated?
Early-stage follicular lymphoma is treated with radiotherapy with the aim of curing it.

More advanced follicular lymphoma tends to behave like a **chronic** illness. This means that it usually flares up from time to time with periods in between when it is less active. Many people live with follicular lymphoma for years and often enjoy pretty good health.

People with follicular lymphoma do not always need treatment straightaway. Instead, doctors may recommend the **watch-and-wait** approach (see pages 50–53). For some people, treatment may not be needed until many months or years later.

When follicular lymphoma needs treatment, most people will have a combination of chemotherapy and antibody therapy. Two commonly used **regimens** are R-CVP and R-CHOP. Bendamustine (Levact®) is another possible drug, which is also given with rituximab.

⟵ You will find more details about R-CVP and R-CHOP on pages 68–69 and about bendamustine on pages 69–70.

5

For people who are less fit, gentler treatment with oral chlorambucil (see page 72), which is often given with prednisolone (see pages 66–67) may be suggested. Rituximab can also be used with chlorambucil, but any benefits must be weighed against the risk of having more side effects and the need to go regularly to a day treatment unit.

Once people are in **remission** after chemotherapy and rituximab, they will most likely be offered **maintenance treatment**. This means having rituximab on its own every 2–3 months for up to 2 years. Maintenance treatment should keep the lymphoma in remission for longer.

⟵ You will find more information about rituximab on pages 72–76.

When follicular lymphoma **relapses** and needs further treatment, doctors usually recommend more chemotherapy. Often, if possible, this will be a different type of chemotherapy. Doctors may also talk to some people about having a stem cell transplant, especially if their lymphoma has relapsed quickly.

For some people there may come a time when their lymphoma stops responding to the gentler treatments or they are not fit enough for more chemotherapy. If this happens, they may be offered treatment with rituximab, or perhaps one of the newer **antibodies**, on its own.

5

Radioimmunotherapy with ^{90}Y-ibritumomab tiuxetan (Zevalin®) may be another possible treatment for some people with follicular lymphoma. It can be given after chemotherapy to make a **remission** last longer. It may also be used for people who have **relapsed** after earlier treatments with chemotherapy and rituximab, or for people with **refractory** lymphoma. In practice it can be given at only a few hospitals in the UK and it is not widely used.

Other, newer targeted therapies, such as idelalisib, ibrutinib and lenalidomide, are being tested in clinical trials. Your doctor will be able to tell you whether there are any suitable clinical trials for you to enter, either in your centre or nearby.

These targeted drugs are likely to be used more in the next few years, either on their own or with other therapies. They usually don't cause too many side effects. Some of them look to be very promising treatments for people with follicular lymphoma.

Chronic lymphocytic leukaemia (CLL)/ small lymphocytic lymphoma (SLL)

What does it mean?

Chronic lymphocytic leukaemia (CLL) and small lymphocytic lymphoma (SLL) are really two forms of the same illness. The same kind of cell (a small **lymphocyte**) has become cancerous in both. The difference is where the cancer cells are found. In CLL most of them are in the blood and **bone marrow**; in SLL they are mainly in the **lymph nodes** and **spleen**.

The word 'leukaemia' means a cancer of blood cells. In this case it is a small lymphocyte that has become cancerous and it behaves as a chronic (long-term) illness.

5

If you have been given this booklet, you will most likely have the SLL form of this illness. You probably have swollen lymph nodes and/or a swollen liver or spleen.

In the following sections, we will not talk about how CLL in the blood and bone marrow only is treated. This type of CLL can be diagnosed on a routine blood test. People often feel well and may be unaware of any problem when they are diagnosed. CLL is also staged in a different way from other low-grade lymphomas.

Who gets it?

CLL/SLL affects adults. Sometimes it can occur in quite young adults, but it is mainly seen in people over the age of 60. It is more common in men.

How will it affect me?
Some people with CLL/SLL have a very slow-growing lymphoma. This means they may have long periods of time when they need no treatment. Other people have a faster-growing form of the lymphoma.

Often, people with CLL/SLL have very few symptoms to start with. Over months or sometimes years, the cancerous cells build up in the bone marrow, blood, spleen, liver and lymph nodes.

This build-up of abnormal cells can cause problems, which may include:

5

- swelling of lymph nodes, often in several places
- flu-like symptoms such as shivering, aching and feeling generally weak
- lots of infections because the **immune system** is not working properly
- damage to your own blood cells by your immune system (known as 'autoimmunity') affecting your **red blood cells** ('autoimmune haemolytic anaemia' or AIHA for short) or your **platelets** ('immune thrombocytopenic purpura' or ITP for short)
- tiredness, weight loss and sweating
- low blood cell counts, usually due to leukaemia cells collecting in the bone marrow or spleen. This can cause **anaemia**, which can make you feel short of breath or very tired. The number of platelets in your blood might also be reduced. This means you are more likely to bleed or bruise very easily.

Sometimes CLL/SLL can change and as time goes on it may grow faster, resulting in **transformation** – often called a 'Richter transformation' or 'Richter syndrome'.

A Richter transformation can grow as fast as many high-grade lymphomas. It needs to be treated with the type of chemotherapy usually given to treat high-grade lymphomas.

How is CLL/SLL treated?

This section talks about treatments for advanced-stage CLL/SLL and not about the treatment of CLL that is just in the bone marrow or blood.

Even if CLL/SLL is classed as being advanced stage, there is rarely any rush to start treatment. Many people who feel well need no treatment, so doctors will often recommend using **watch and wait** (see pages 50–53).

5

First-line treatment for people with CLL/SLL who do have symptoms or feel unwell usually involves chemotherapy. Often this will be given with an **antibody** and/or steroids too.

If you are fit enough you may be offered a treatment known as FCR (see page 70). If your doctors do not think FCR is the best treatment for you, other possible treatments include:
- chlorambucil
- bendamustine.

Chlorambucil (see page 72) works well for some people, especially those with a mild form of the lymphoma. It causes fewer side effects than other kinds of chemotherapy, making it a good choice for people who might not cope with a stronger treatment. It can be given for up to 12 months.

A recent trial has suggested people given the antibody obinutuzumab (see page 75) along with chlorambucil are likely to have a longer **remission**. Obinutuzumab needs to be given intravenously and does have some extra side effects, so its benefits still need to be weighed up carefully. At the time of writing, the treatment is yet to be approved by NICE (National Institute for Health and Care Excellence), so it is not yet widely available.

Bendamustine (see pages 69–70) is another possible drug that is being used more often in a number of lymphomas. It is available within the NHS to treat certain people with CLL.

5

Maintenance therapy with rituximab is not usually given to people with CLL/SLL – it does not appear to work as well as in other low-grade lymphomas. There are, however, trials now looking at the use of the antibody ofatumumab (see page 75) as maintenance therapy in CLL. Other newer drugs may possibly also work well as maintenance therapy, so this is an area that may change in future.

Treatment for CLL/SLL that has relapsed will again depend on how fit someone is – there are a number of possible choices. Another of the treatments mentioned above may be tried, although some of the gentler treatments can also be used again. If you did not have rituximab as part of your first treatment, you may be given FCR when your lymphoma comes back.

Alemtuzumab (MabCampath®, sometimes just called Campath) is another antibody that may be used to treat a few people with CLL/SLL.

Alemtuzumab can work well when someone has CLL cells mainly in their blood and bone marrow. It is not good at shrinking down very large lymph nodes. It may be given to some people who have not responded to chemotherapy that includes fludarabine – especially if their CLL cells show a change affecting their genes known as 'deletion 17p'.

Ofatumumab (Arzerra®), another newer antibody, has been used for people with CLL/SLL that is **refractory** or has **relapsed** after treatment with fludarabine and alemtuzumab. It can also be used for people who aren't able to receive these treatments.

Although this treatment has been licensed, it was not approved by NICE, who also look at the cost of treatments. However, at the time of writing, doctors in England can ask the Cancer Drugs Fund to pay for ofatumumab for certain people.

Ibrutinib and idelalisib (see pages 77–78) are other new targeted therapies that look very promising in CLL/SLL. The cell signal pathways they target are important in the growth of CLL cells. They may work better than the standard treatments in people with CLL cells that show certain changes affecting their genes.

Ibrutinib has been used in trials on its own but its use with other drugs is also now being tested. Idelalisib has been used with rituximab in trials for people with relapsed CLL/SLL.

Steroids (often prednisolone) are also used in treating CLL/SLL (see pages 66–67).

5

Steroids may be given:
- before starting other chemotherapy treatment – for instance, if your bone marrow is not working well steroids may improve your **blood count**
- to treat autoimmune haemolytic anaemia (AIHA) or immune thrombocytopenic purpura (ITP) – the steroids help to 'damp down' the attack from your immune system
- instead of alemtuzumab or ofatumumab or together with other drugs for people who have lymphoma that is hard to treat with standard therapy.

5

A stem cell transplant is sometimes offered to people who are younger, especially if their CLL/SLL has relapsed or is growing more quickly than normal. Stem cell transplants aim to give people a longer **remission** than chemotherapy alone would. Transplants can be either **autologous** (using your own cells) or **allogeneic** (using a donor's cells). An allogeneic transplant may be able to cure a few people with CLL/SLL, but for many people they carry too many risks and side effects.

If you would like to know more about whether a transplant may be suitable for you, you should talk to your consultant or nurse specialist.

Marginal zone lymphomas

Marginal zone lymphomas make up around 1 in 10 of all non-Hodgkin lymphomas. They all develop from the same kind of cell, a 'marginal zone **B cell**'. These cells are normally seen in areas called the marginal zone, which are found in **lymph nodes** and other parts of the lymphatic system.

Marginal zone lymphomas can grow in many different places and are often **extranodal**, meaning they grow in areas outside the lymphatic system.

There are different types of marginal zone lymphoma:
- MALT lymphoma, which can occur in the stomach or in other areas
- splenic marginal zone lymphoma
- nodal marginal zone lymphoma – the least common type.

MALT lymphoma and splenic marginal zone lymphoma are quite different from other low-grade lymphomas. The best treatments for them are also often quite different.

5

Over the next few pages you will find separate sections on each type of marginal zone lymphoma. We again suggest you read only about your own type of lymphoma, at least at first.

Gastric MALT lymphoma

What does it mean?
MALT stands for **m**ucosa-**a**ssociated **l**ymphoid **t**issue (a mucosa or mucous membrane is a soft, moist lining found in certain areas inside the body).

MALT lymphomas are extranodal marginal zone B-cell lymphomas. They begin to grow in the mucous membranes. Gastric MALT lymphoma grows in the lining of the stomach, which is the most common place to find a MALT lymphoma.

Who gets it?

MALT lymphomas make up less than 1 in 10 of all B-cell non-Hodgkin lymphomas. They can occur at any age, but typically affect older adults.

Gastric MALT lymphoma is linked to infection with the **bacteria** *Helicobacter pylori*. This infection is known to cause 'gastritis' or inflammation in the lining of the stomach. The inflammation leads to a build-up of **lymphocytes**. In some people, over time the lymphocytes become cancerous and a lymphoma develops.

How will it affect me?

People with MALT lymphoma in the stomach usually have symptoms of indigestion. Some people may feel sick or have abdominal pain. They may also have lost weight, but fevers and sweating are less common than in other types of lymphoma.

Gastric MALT lymphoma is often diagnosed after an endoscopy. This test involves looking into the oesophagus (gullet) and stomach with a special tiny camera carried at the tip of a flexible tube. If the lining of the stomach looks abnormal, a **biopsy** will be taken so a **pathologist** can look at it under the microscope. Sometimes more tests have to be done on the biopsy, so the final result can take 2–3 weeks.

How is it treated?

In many people, gastric MALT lymphoma will be found only in the stomach. In this case, treatment with antibiotics is usually tried first. These aim to get rid of the *Helicobacter pylori* infection. Once this has gone, the lymphoma will often start to shrink. Further endoscopies are usually done to see if the lymphoma is getting better. This can take anything from a few months to a year or more.

Around three-quarters of people treated with antibiotics will see an improvement in their lymphoma. If your lymphoma doesn't respond to this kind of treatment, or if it has spread beyond the lining of the stomach, you may need other treatments. These could include chemotherapy, often with tablets, together with antibody therapy, or radiotherapy. Surgery is not a good treatment for this type of lymphoma.

Sometimes treatment will not get rid of all the lymphoma cells and stomach biopsies will still be abnormal. If, however, the lymphoma is not causing symptoms and the stomach looks normal on endoscopy, a **watch-and-wait** approach (see pages 50–53) may be suitable. More treatment will be recommended if ulcers are seen or if the lymphoma causes symptoms.

Non-gastric MALT lymphoma

What does it mean?
MALT stands for **m**ucosa-**a**ssociated **l**ymphoid **t**issue (a mucosa or mucous membrane is a soft, moist lining found in certain areas inside the body). MALT lymphomas are **extranodal** marginal zone B-cell lymphomas. They begin to grow in the mucous membranes. Non-gastric MALT lymphomas can grow almost anywhere in the body. They are most common in the thyroid gland, salivary glands, skin, lung, breast, bowel, tear glands or other parts of the eye.

Who gets it?

MALT lymphomas make up less than 1 in 10 of all B-cell non-Hodgkin lymphomas. They can occur at any age, but typically affect older adults.

MALT lymphomas are more likely to occur in people who have had certain illnesses or infections. For example:

- MALT lymphoma of the thyroid gland is more common in people who have had an illness called Hashimoto's thyroiditis.
- MALT lymphoma in the salivary glands or lung is more common in people with Sjögren syndrome.
- Infection with *Chlamydia psittaci* is linked with lymphoma in the tear gland or around the eye.
- Infection with *Campylobacter jejuni* is linked with lymphoma in the bowel.
- Infection with *Borrelia burgdorferi*, which causes Lyme disease, is linked with lymphoma in the skin.

How will it affect me?

The symptoms of non-gastric MALT lymphoma will depend on what part of your body is affected. The lymphoma may be found only in the tissue where it first started to grow. In other cases it can spread further or involve the **lymph nodes** and **bone marrow**, but this is less common than with other lymphomas. MALT lymphomas are also less likely to cause other common symptoms of lymphoma such as weight loss, fevers and night sweats.

MALT lymphoma often causes a lump, and/or irritation and soreness in the area where it is growing. MALT lymphoma in the lung may cause a cough or shortness

5

of breath. When it is in the tear gland, it will make the eye red and watery; in the thyroid it may cause a hoarse voice or problems swallowing; and in the skin it appears as one or more small, reddish swellings.

How is it treated?

The treatment of MALT lymphoma will depend on the part of the body involved. If it may be linked to an infection, antibiotics will usually be given to treat this.

In some cases, if the **biopsy** has removed all of the lymphoma that could be seen, further treatment may not be needed until more problems occur. This approach is known as **watch and wait** (see pages 50–53).

5

If the MALT lymphoma has not all been removed or is in more than one area, other treatments may be needed. These could include radiotherapy and/or chemotherapy, which is often given with the **antibody** rituximab.

 If you would like to find out more about MALT lymphoma please ring our helpline (0808 808 5555) or see our website (www.lymphomas.org.uk).

Splenic marginal zone lymphoma

What does it mean?

Splenic marginal zone lymphoma usually begins to grow in the **spleen**. The spleen is part of the **immune system** and it also helps to remove old blood cells.

You might also hear it called 'splenic lymphoma with villous lymphocytes'. This is because the lymphoma cells are sometimes found in the bloodstream. Doctors describe the **lymphocytes** seen under a microscope in this type of lymphoma as 'villous', meaning they look 'hairy'.

Who gets it?
Splenic marginal zone lymphoma occurs more often in older people. It is less common than MALT lymphoma.

In some people splenic marginal zone lymphoma may be linked to infection with the hepatitis C **virus**.

How will it affect me?
Splenic marginal zone lymphoma is a slow-growing lymphoma. It often causes the spleen to slowly swell, which doctors call **splenomegaly**.

Having a swollen spleen can give you abdominal pain. It can also leave you with too few blood cells. This is because one of the jobs of your spleen is to remove old blood cells and a swollen spleen may remove too many.

This can result in:
• **anaemia**, which may make you feel short of breath or very tired
• a fall in the number of **platelets** in your blood, which means you are more likely to bleed or bruise easily.

Splenic lymphoma may be found just in the spleen. It can also spread to involve other tissues, such as the bone marrow. If your **bone marrow** is affected, this can also make you short of blood cells. Sometimes the lymphoma cells from the bone marrow are also seen in the bloodstream. **Lymph nodes** are not often involved in this type of lymphoma.

5

Very occasionally the lymphoma cells produce a small amount of an abnormal **protein** known as a 'globulin'. This can be found in the bloodstream. It can make the blood thicker on testing in the laboratory but this rarely causes any problems.

How is it treated?

Splenic lymphoma may be treated in different ways. Some people may need no treatment for a while, an approach known as **watch and wait** (see pages 50–53).

If blood tests show signs of hepatitis C infection, antiviral treatment will probably be given. This may lead to an improvement in the lymphoma too.

5

If you need treatment, you may be offered antibody therapy. Rituximab on its own (see pages 72–76) is a very good treatment for splenic marginal zone lymphoma. Chemotherapy, often with tablets, may also be suggested for some people.

For other people, removing the spleen by surgery may help, especially if the swollen spleen is causing lots of symptoms. This operation, which is known as a **splenectomy**, can sometimes be done laparoscopically (by keyhole surgery). If your spleen is removed, you can still live quite normally but you will have a higher risk of some infections. Because of this you will need to have certain vaccinations before your surgery and should take a small dose of protective antibiotics afterwards.

 For more information about splenectomy please ring our helpline (0808 808 5555) or see our website (www.lymphomas.org.uk).

Nodal marginal zone lymphoma

What does it mean?
This type of lymphoma develops in **lymph nodes** only. There is no sign of lymphoma in the spleen or other organs.

Who gets it?
Nodal marginal zone lymphoma is an uncommon lymphoma – it causes fewer than 1 in 50 non-Hodgkin lymphomas. It is most often seen in older adults but can occasionally occur in children, when it is much commoner in boys.

5

In some people, nodal marginal zone lymphoma may be linked to infection with the hepatitis C **virus**.

How will it affect me?
Most people with this lymphoma go to their doctor with one or more swollen lymph nodes, which are not usually painful. Some people may feel very tired, but loss of weight, fevers and sweating affect only a few people. This type of lymphoma is only **diagnosed** when no lymphoma can be found outside the lymph nodes.

How is it treated?
Nodal marginal zone lymphoma is often treated in a similar way to follicular lymphoma. It does not always need treatment straightaway, an approach known as **watch and wait** (see pages 50–53).

If the lymphoma is in one area of the body only, it may be treated with radiotherapy. Sometimes this can cure the lymphoma. Nodal marginal zone lymphoma is, however, often more widespread when it is diagnosed.

When treatment is needed for advanced-stage lymphoma, chemotherapy, with or without rituximab, is used. This might include CVP, CHOP, fludarabine or gentler chlorambucil treatment. Some people might also be offered high-dose chemotherapy and a stem cell transplant, for instance if their lymphoma **relapses** quickly.

⬅ You will find more information about these different types of chemotherapy on pages 68–72.

5

The treatment your doctors recommend for you will depend on many things. Talk to your doctors about this treatment and why they feel it is best for you.

Lymphoplasmacytic lymphoma (Waldenström's macroglobulinaemia)

What does it mean?
'Lymphoplasmacytic' describes how the cells in this type of lymphoma look under the microscope. It means the **lymphocytes** look a bit more like cells called 'plasma cells', which produce antibodies.

The name 'Waldenström's macroglobulinaemia' is also sometimes used instead. Dr Jan Waldenström was the doctor who first described the condition in 1948. 'Macroglobulinaemia' means that the blood contains a large abnormal **protein**, which is produced by the lymphoma cells.

Who gets it?

Lymphoplasmactyic lymphoma is an uncommon type of lymphoma. It is found mainly in people who are over 65.

Some people with this condition have relatives with the same or a similar condition. This suggests there may be a genetic tendency towards this condition within the wider family (in the same way some families might have a tendency to heart disease). It is not normally inherited from parent to child and at present doctors don't recommend checking other family members.

How will it affect me?

Lymphoplasmacytic lymphoma grows slowly and may not cause many symptoms. It is sometimes found by chance in people who feel well.

The lymphoma cells are almost always found in the **bone marrow** and may be seen in the bloodstream too. They may cause some swelling of the **spleen** but swollen **lymph nodes** are less common than in other types of lymphoma.

Lymphoma in your bone marrow and spleen may lead to low blood cell counts, causing:
- **anaemia**, which can make you feel short of breath or very tired
- a fall in the number of **platelets** in your blood, which means you are more likely to bleed or bruise easily.

In lymphoplasmacytic lymphoma the cells usually produce abnormal proteins ('globulins') that can be found in the bloodstream. There are different kinds of globulins. The one found most often in this type of

5

lymphoma is the IgM globulin, which is the largest. Because of their size these globulins make the blood thicker. Doctors measure how thick your blood is with a test called the 'plasma viscosity' – a higher result means your blood is thicker.

If your blood is very thick, it may cause a problem known as 'hyperviscosity'. This makes it very hard for your blood to pass through any small blood vessels. It can cause a number of problems, including:

- nosebleeds
- confusion, sleepiness or poor concentration
- dizziness or headaches
- blurred vision or loss of vision
- shortness of breath.

5

Sometimes the abnormal globulin can affect the nerves to the hands and the feet (known as 'neuropathy', see pages 62–63). This may cause weakness, tingling or numbness of the fingers or toes.

In other people, in colder parts of the body the abnormal globulins can clump together or make red blood cells stick together. This can cause problems with blood flow to the hands, feet and nose, or may affect the skin and kidneys.

People with lymphoplasmacytic lymphoma may lose weight sometimes but problems with fevers and night sweats tend to be less common. They may also find they easily pick up infections or have trouble getting rid of them.

In a small number of people with lymphoplasmacytic lymphoma the cells can become larger and start to grow more rapidly over time. This **transformation** of the lymphoma makes it behave more like a high-grade lymphoma. If this happens you will need to be treated with a type of chemotherapy regimen more often used for high-grade lymphoma.

How is it treated?

Lymphoplasmacytic lymphoma can be treated in many different ways.

If you have no symptoms or just a few symptoms from your lymphoma, you may not need any treatment at first. In this case your doctors will suggest the **watch-and-wait** approach (see pages 50–53).

People who do need treatment are usually given chemotherapy, often along with an **antibody** and a steroid such as dexamethasone. There are lots of choices, which range from chlorambucil – the most gentle treatment – to stronger **regimens** that include drugs such as cyclophosphamide, bendamustine and fludarabine (see pages 68–72). Another drug sometimes included in regimens to treat this lymphoma is bortezomib (see pages 77–79).

Rituximab (see pages 72–76) is often used as treatment for lymphoplasmacytic lymphoma, usually along with chemotherapy drugs. It must be used carefully though as it can sometimes make the blood thicker when it is first given.

If you have problems due to hyperviscosity, a treatment called 'plasmapheresis' (sometimes called 'plasma exchange') can be used. This treatment can quickly

5

remove some of the abnormal proteins from your blood, which allows it to flow better.

Plasmapheresis treatment usually takes a few hours. During this time you will have a cannula (a plastic tube that goes into a vein) placed in each arm and will be connected to a special machine. The machine takes blood out of one arm and separates this into the plasma (the liquid part) and the cells. The plasma, which contains the abnormal protein, is removed. The cells are returned through your other arm along with some replacement plasma to make up your normal amount of blood.

5

This treatment is most often needed to 'buy time' before chemotherapy has taken effect. Its effect is short-lived as the proteins build up again in the bloodstream if the lymphoma is still active.

Stem cell transplants are sometimes offered to people who are younger, especially if their lymphoma has relapsed quickly or is causing other problems. Stem cell transplants aim to give people a longer **remission** than chemotherapy alone would. They can be either **autologous** (using your own cells) or **allogeneic** (using a donor's cells). An allogeneic transplant may be able to cure a few people, but for many people this kind of transplant carries too many risks and side effects.

Newer, targeted therapies, including ibrutinib and idelalisib, are also being used in clinical trials. You might like to ask your doctor whether there is a clinical trial (see pages 35–36) that you could take part in.

Cutaneous lymphoma

Some low-grade non-Hodgkin lymphomas begin in the skin and some of these may never affect other areas. Lymphoma in the skin is known as cutaneous lymphoma. It can develop from either **B cells** or **T cells**. The most common type is a T-cell lymphoma called mycosis fungoides.

Cutaneous lymphomas are more common in men, particularly between the ages of 50 and 70, but men and women of all ages can develop these lymphomas.

Cutaneous lymphomas are quite different from other lymphomas in how they behave and what tests are needed to diagnose them. Sometimes, they can be hard to diagnose because they often look like much more common skin conditions such as psoriasis or eczema.

The way they are treated is often very different too. The treatment needed will depend on how the skin is affected and on whether the lymphoma is affecting other parts of the body, such as lymph nodes. Possible treatments include ultraviolet light treatment, steroid creams, radiotherapy and chemotherapy.

 We produce information specifically about skin (cutaneous) lymphomas and their treatment. Please ring our helpline (0808 808 5555) or see our website (www.lymphomas.org.uk) if you would like a copy of any of this information or want to talk more about this type of lymphoma.

Looking after yourself

Your feelings

Helping yourself

When someone close to you has lymphoma

6

Your feelings

No one can say exactly how you will feel when you learn you have low-grade lymphoma, when you are on watch and wait or having treatment, or even afterwards. You will probably have all sorts of different feelings at different times. This is quite normal as there is no right or wrong way to handle things.

These are some of the feelings you may have:
- shock – you may feel numb and find it hard to accept things at first
- anxiety – you may be worried about your disease, your treatment, your future or your family
- sadness – it may be that your life and plans, at least for a time, are going to have to change
- fear – often this is fear of the unknown, so finding out more about what to expect can help
- anger – you may feel you've lost all control of your life and resent the fact that this has happened to you.

These feelings are all normal. It is important to accept them and give yourself time to deal with them. It's also important to talk about your feelings, especially if there are times when you are finding it harder to cope.

Talking to someone close to you can sometimes be hard if they are dealing with their own feelings about your illness too. Your nurse specialist is often a good person to talk with or there may be specialist counsellors available at your hospital. Our helpline staff are ready to listen too (0808 808 5555). They may also be able to put you in touch with one of our 'buddies', who have all been affected by lymphoma too.

6

'A diagnosis of cancer is a thing that can set you on a marooned island inside your own head. Trying to act like it's no big thing can test a person beyond what is do-able day to day.'

Depression
You may feel that there are times when you don't want to talk and just want to be alone. This is quite normal but if you start to feel this all the time, it could be a sign of depression.

People who are depressed may also feel hopeless, guilty or worthless. They may have no interest in hobbies or normal activities and often find they wake very early or are sleeping all the time.

If you, or those around you, think you might be depressed, talk to someone about this. Depression will get worse if you don't do anything about it, but it can be successfully treated.

'Lymphoma used to be the first thing I thought about, but now it is only in the back of my mind and I am able to lead my normal life.'

When you are not on active treatment
One of the things many people with low-grade lymphoma find hardest to accept is that their lymphoma does not always need treating. People sometimes feel they are just waiting for their lymphoma to come back or start causing them problems.

It often takes time to understand what it all means, and why your doctor is not doing anything to treat you. Learning more about your lymphoma can help you understand the reasons for either doing something or not doing anything. This can help you feel more in control and confident in what is happening.

If you are someone who finds it hard to cope with not being on treatment, remember you are not alone. Be honest about your feelings, talk to people and seek help. You could:

- speak to your hospital team, who may be able to offer more support and an explanation as to why you are on watch and wait
- call our helpline, who are always happy to talk or may be able to put you in touch with one of our 'buddies' who is, or has been, on watch and wait
- join a local support group where you are likely to meet other people who know about watch and wait
- take a look at our website forums to see what other people have felt and said about being on watch and wait.

 If you would like to talk about watch and wait or find out about our buddy scheme, please ring our helpline (0808 808 5555) or visit our website (www.lymphomas.org.uk).

After you have finished a course of treatment
Very mixed feelings may also affect those who have already been given treatment. In fact some people feel more anxious and depressed once their treatment is finished, even if it has been successful.

If this happens to you, it may be because you:
- know your lymphoma is likely to come back and find it hard to put this out of your mind
- are still recovering from your treatment – sometimes side effects such as fatigue can last for months
- start to think deeply about what has happened only once your treatment is finished
- have had to make changes to your life because of the lymphoma or its treatment
- are worried about the future and find it hard to plan ahead.

It is important to realise that these feeling are all normal, but getting on with your life can still be hard. Talk to people, including your GP and hospital team, about how you are really feeling. Let them know too if you still have any side effects or symptoms.

Our helpline staff and our 'buddies', who can understand how your are feeling, are also still there to listen when you are not on active treatment (0808 808 5555).

Helping yourself

There are many things you can do to help yourself if you have non-Hodgkin lymphoma. These are a few suggestions.

Look after your general health and fitness
Although there is no scientific proof, making changes to your lifestyle may well help you get through any future treatment more easily. Changes that you make now may help you live a healthier and fuller life.

You may wish to think about:

- stopping smoking – lung infections are more common both with chemotherapy and with smoking
- limiting your alcohol intake
- eating a healthy diet
- losing weight if you're heavier than you should be
- taking regular exercise – research has shown that exercise can help reduce fatigue, as well as being good for your body generally
- visiting your dentist regularly – a healthy mouth can reduce your risk of infection when having chemotherapy.

Your GP or hospital team can offer you advice on what would be sensible and most important for you.

6

'Life takes on a new perspective after diagnosis. Time helps you to get your head round things and kind of makes you prioritise what is really important.'

People often find that having a serious illness makes them look again at their lifestyle. This might include other aspects of your life, such as your responsibilities, your job or finances and how you spend your time too. Many people find having lymphoma makes them value the simple things in life, such as spending time with family and friends and doing the activities they enjoy.

 Our booklet *Living with lymphoma* gives more information on looking after yourself and about day-to-day life with lymphoma. If you would like a copy please ring our helpline (0808 808 5555) or see our website (www.lymphomas.org.uk).

Find out about your lymphoma

Knowing more about your illness and your treatments can help in a number of ways, for example by:

- easing some of the fears and anxieties you may have
- picking up tips to avoid or reduce problems during and after treatment
- knowing how to deal with any side effects
- knowing when to call the hospital if a problem occurs
- helping you feel more in control of what is happening to you.

When someone close to you has lymphoma

When someone close to you has lymphoma it can be a hard time for you too. You may feel helpless watching the person you love going through all the tests and treatment. You may feel you don't know what to do or how to help.

There are lots of things you will be able to do, but don't forget to take care of yourself too. Make sure you look after your own health, particularly if you already have any illnesses, eat well and try to get plenty of rest. You will go through many of the same feelings as your loved one and will need time to deal with these too. Talk to someone if you are finding it hard to cope.

People sometimes worry that they don't know what to say or will say the wrong thing. In fact, just being there, ready to listen, is often a huge help. Let the person know that you love and care for them, in whatever way you can – a smile or a hug may say much more than any words.

'My advice is just deal with each day in your own way, there will be good ones and not so good ones, but it does get easier.'

Practical things that may help your friend or loved one include:
- providing transport to hospital
- going along to hospital appointments with them to help remember what has been said
- helping with shopping or preparing meals
- taking care of other family members
- encouraging them to spend time seeing other people or doing something they enjoy
- organising fun things to do when they feel up to it.

6

→ You might like to contact Carers UK, who can offer more free information, help and support. You will find their details on page 133.

Key facts

There is no right or wrong way to feel about having low-grade non-Hodgkin lymphoma. You will probably feel a mixture of shock, anxiety, sadness, fear and anger at different times.

If you, or those around you, think you may be depressed, talk to someone about this. Depression can be treated.

Finding out more about your illness and treatments can help you know what to expect and how to deal with problems. This can also help you feel more in control of what is happening to you.

Many people find having a serious illness makes them think about whether they need to change their lifestyle. Some changes could help you get through further treatment more easily or might help you to live a fuller and healthier life.

If someone close to you has lymphoma, there are lots of practical things you can do to help, as well as ways to offer support. It is important though that you take care of yourself too and talk to someone if you are finding it hard to cope.

6

Help and support

Whatever your situation, we hope that this booklet has helped you to understand more about low-grade non-Hodgkin lymphoma, particularly the type that is most relevant to you, and the sort of treatments your doctors are likely to recommend.

If you would like further information about anything mentioned in this booklet, or would like to talk to someone, please get in touch with us.

How we can help

Helpline – The Lymphoma Association helpline is there to offer a listening ear for you, your family and friends. Your call will be confidential and free. Please ring us on 0808 808 5555 if you would like to talk about any aspect of lymphoma or about how you are feeling. Our helpline is open from Monday to Friday (please see our website for the current opening hours). You can also email the helpline on information@lymphomas.org.uk or contact them via Live Chat on our website.

Lymphoma Association buddy scheme – Many people feel more encouraged and supported after speaking to other people affected by lymphoma. Even if their experience was not exactly the same as yours, it can be a relief to speak with someone who has been through something similar. We may be able to put you in touch by telephone or email with one of our buddies.

Lymphoma Association support groups – There are support groups for people with lymphoma around the UK. Please ring our helpline for more information or use the 'search' facility on our website to find your nearest group.

Online – We have forums on our website where you can share what has happened to you. We are also on Facebook, Twitter and YouTube.

Lymphoma matters – You can subscribe to our free quarterly magazine, which is full of up-to-date information about lymphoma, reports on the latest research and new treatments, articles on living with lymphoma and interviews with people affected by lymphoma.

Free information – We have lots of information on lymphoma and its treatment on our website (www.lymphomas.org.uk). We also produce a series of booklets about lymphoma. These can be downloaded or ordered from our website and are all free of charge. You can also ask for booklets to be sent to you by ringing our helpline on 0808 808 5555 or by email (information@lymphomas.org.uk).

How you can help us

We continually strive to improve our information resources for people affected by lymphoma and we would be interested in any feedback you might have on this booklet. Please visit www.lymphomas.org.uk/feedback or email publications@lymphomas.org.uk if you have any comments. Or, if you prefer, please ring our helpline on 0808 808 5555.

Glossary

Allogeneic the use of someone else's tissue (eg stem cells)

Anaemia lack of red blood cells in the blood, often talked about as the level of haemoglobin

Anaesthetic drugs given to make a part of the body numb (a local anaesthetic) or put the whole body to sleep (a general anaesthetic)

Antibody a protein that sticks to disease-causing cells or organisms, such as bacteria, leading to their death

Autologous the use of a person's own tissue (eg stem cells)

B cell the same as a B lymphocyte, a white blood cell that normally helps to fight infections by making antibodies

Bacteria small organisms, some of which can cause infections and disease

Biopsy a test that takes some cells to be looked at under a microscope; taking out a whole lymph node is called an **excision biopsy** and using a special needle to take a smaller sample is a **core biopsy**

Blood count   a blood test that counts the cells in your blood, including the red blood cells, the different kinds of white blood cells, and platelets

Bone marrow   spongy material at the centre of some of our bones that produces the body's blood cells

Chronic   something that is long term and doesn't ever fully go away

Cure   the lymphoma has been treated to the point where it has gone and will not come back in the future

Cycle   a block of chemotherapy that is followed by a rest period to allow the healthy normal cells to recover

Diagnosis   deciding what an illness or disease is; giving it a name

Diaphragm   a sheet of muscle that separates the chest from the abdomen (see picture on page 10)

Extranodal   refers to a lymphoma that forms in an area outside the lymphatic system

Haematologist   a doctor who specialises in diseases of the blood and blood cells

HIV   human immunodeficiency virus, a virus that causes weakness in part of the immune system that can lead to AIDS (acquired immune deficiency syndrome)

Immune system	the parts of the body that fight off and prevent infection
Intravenous	into a vein
Lymphocyte	a type of white blood cell that normally helps to fight infections; may be either a B lymphocyte or a T lymphocyte
Lymph node	gland that acts like a sieve in the lymphatic system; involved in fighting infection
Maintenance treatment	treatment given with the aim of keeping the lymphoma in remission for longer
Neutropenia	a lack of neutrophils in the blood, which makes you prone to infection
Neutrophil	a type of white blood cell that is important in fighting infections caused by bacteria or fungus
Oncologist	a doctor who specialises in treating cancer
Pathologist	a doctor who looks at and tests diseased tissues to make a diagnosis
Platelets	the tiny fragments of cells in your blood that help form blood clots and stop bleeding
Protein	matter found in living things with many roles, including helping to control how our cells work and fighting infections
Radiographer	a person who takes X-rays or gives radiotherapy

Radiologist   a doctor who can analyse X-rays and scans

Radiotherapist   a doctor who specialises in radiotherapy (also often known as a clinical oncologist)

Red blood cell   a cell that contains the red pigment haemoglobin, which allows it to carry oxygen around the body

Refractory   meaning an illness that has not responded well to treatment

Regimen   a combination of drugs given together in a set pattern

Relapse   to come back after remission or to flare up after a quiet period

Remission   the lymphoma has been controlled by treatment

Spleen   an organ about the size of a closed fist behind the stomach that is part of the immune system

Splenectomy   an operation to remove the spleen, sometimes done laparoscopically (by keyhole surgery)

Splenomegaly   a term meaning that the spleen is larger than normal

Subcutaneous   underneath the skin

Symptom   something you notice or feel when you have an illness

T cell	the same as a T lymphocyte, a white blood cell that normally helps to fight infections caused by viruses
Thrombo-cytopenia	a lack of platelets in the blood, which makes you more prone to bleeding or bruising
Transformation	change to a faster-growing (high-grade) lymphoma
Virus	a tiny organism that often causes infection and disease
Watch and wait	also known as active monitoring, a policy of delaying treatment in someone who feels relatively well until their symptoms become harder to live with
White blood cell	a cell found in the blood and in many other tissues that helps our bodies to fight infections; there are several different kinds, including lymphocytes and neutrophils

Useful organisations

This is a short list of useful organisations, but there are many others. If you can't find the right organisation listed here, please ring our helpline (0808 808 5555).

British Association for Counselling and Psychotherapy
Has a register of accredited counsellors throughout the UK.
☎ 01455 883300
www.bacp.co.uk
✉ bacp@bacp.co.uk

Cancer Research UK
Offers information and statistics on all types of cancer, including treatment, prevention, screening and research. A team of specialist cancer nurses can be contacted by phone by calling their Freephone number.
☎ 0808 800 4040 (Monday–Friday, 9am–5pm)
www.cancerresearchuk.org/cancer-help
✉ via website

Carers UK
Offers free and confidential information for carers.
☎ 0808 808 7777
www.carersuk.org
✉ via website

CLL Support Association
Offers information and support to those affected by CLL.
☎ 0800 977 4396
www.cllsupport.org.uk
✉ info@cllsupport.org.uk

Depression Alliance

Offers information about the symptoms and treatment of depression, national and local groups.

☎ 0845 123 2320

www.depressionalliance.org

✉ information@depressionalliance.org

Infertility Network UK

Gives information and emotional support to those affected by infertility.

☎ 0800 008 7464 (Monday–Thursday, 9am–4pm)

www.infertilitynetworkuk.com

✉ via website

Leukaemia & Lymphoma Research

Funds research into the causes and treatment of leukaemia, lymphoma and related diseases.

☎ 020 7504 2200 (Monday–Friday, 9am–5pm)

www.leukaemialymphomaresearch.org.uk

✉ info@beatingbloodcancers.org.uk

Macmillan Cancer Support

Offers practical, medical, emotional and financial support to people living with cancer.

☎ 0808 808 0000 (Monday–Friday, 9am–8pm)

www.macmillan.org.uk

✉ via website

Maggie's Cancer Caring Centres

Offers a network of drop-in centres throughout the UK (as well as an 'online' centre) with the aim of supporting people with cancer, their family and friends.

☏ 0300 123 1801

www.maggiescentres.org

✉ enquiries@maggiescentres.org

WMUK

UK point of contact for people with Waldenström's macroglobulinaemia. They have an online forum and run an annual national seminar for patients.

☏ 0117 3735 733

www.wmuk.org.uk

✉ via website

Selected references

The full list of references is available on request. Please contact us via email (publications@lymphomas.org.uk) or telephone 01296 619409 if you would like a copy.

Books
Swerdlow SH, et al (eds). *WHO Classification of tumours of haematopoietic and lymphoid tissues*. 2008. IARC, Lyon.

Hatton C, et al. *Lymphoma*. 2008. Health Press: Oxford.

Journal articles
Ardeshna KM, et al. Rituximab versus a watch-and-wait approach in patients with advanced-stage, asymptomatic, non-bulky follicular lymphoma: an open-label randomised phase 3 trial. *Lancet Oncology*, 2014. 15: 424–435.

Gopal AK, et al. PI3Kδ inhibition by idelalisib in patients with relapsed indolent lymphoma. *New England Journal of Medicine*, 2014. 370: 1008–1018.

Kostakoglu L, Cheson BD. State-of-the-art research on "lymphomas: role of molecular imaging for staging, prognostic evaluation, and treatment response". *Frontiers in Oncology*, 2013. 3: 212.

Rummel MJ, et al. Bendamustine plus rituximab versus CHOP plus rituximab as first-line treatment for patients with indolent and mantle-cell lymphomas: an open-label, multicentre, randomised, phase 3 non-inferiority trial. *Lancet*, 2013. 381: 1203–1210.

Ujjani C, Cheson BD. The current status and future impact of targeted therapies in non-Hodgkin lymphoma. *Expert Reviews in Hematology*, 2013. 6: 191–203.

Joshi M, et al. Marginal zone lymphoma: old, new, targeted, and epigenetic therapies. *Therapeutic Advances in Hematology*, 2012. 3: 275–290.

Lunning M, Vose JM. Management of indolent lymphoma: Where are we now and where are we going? *Blood Reviews*, 2012. 26: 279–288.

McNamara C, et al. Guidelines on the investigation and management of follicular lymphoma. *British Journal of Haematology*, 2012. 156: 446–467.

Oscier D, et al. Guidelines on the diagnosis, investigation and management of chronic lymphocytic leukaemia. *British Journal of Haematology*, 2012. 159: 541–564.

Zinzani PL. The many faces of marginal zone lymphoma. *Hematology/The American Society of Hematology Education Program*, 2012. 2012: 426–432.

Other sources
Cancer Research UK. *UK cancer incidence statistics 2011*. Available at: www.cancerresearchuk.org/cancer-info/cancerstats/types/nhl (accessed August 2014).

Appendix:
Tips for coping with treatment side effects

The following information suggests possible ways of dealing with side effects. It covers only some of the most common ideas – be sure to ask your medical team for advice about dealing with your side effects.

Generally speaking you should tell your team if you feel unwell in any way.

 For more information about dealing with specific side effects please call us on 0808 808 5555.

Low white cell count (neutropenia)

Call the hospital **at once** if you develop signs of infection, such as fever, temperature of 38°C or above, chills, shivering and sweating.

 Other possible signs of infection are listed on page 59.

The following tips may help you lower your risk of developing an infection:

Wash well and regularly. Wash hands before meals, after using the toilet, after using public facilities.

Avoid places that could increase your risk of infection, such as swimming pools, crowded shops and buses.

Avoid contact with people who have infections (including chickenpox).

Don't eat anything that is past its sell-by date and eat refrigerated food within 24 hours once it has been opened.

Avoid foods that contain lots of live bacteria. These include:

- unpasteurised cheeses
- takeaways
- raw or undercooked eggs
- live or probiotic yoghurt (pasteurised yoghurt is fine)
- peppercorns
- undercooked meats and fish
- pâté.

Ask your nurse for information on 'clean' or 'safe' diets.

Take care when handling pets – avoid bites or scratches and wash your hands afterwards. If possible, ask someone else to deal with litter trays and pet faeces.

Wear gloves for gardening.

Low red cell count (anaemia)

Tell your doctor if you feel short of breath, abnormally tired or dizzy, or have abnormal aches and pains.

Ask about what treatment you might have for anaemia.

Low platelet count (thrombocytopenia)

Tell your hospital team about bruising and bleeding. Call the hospital at once if you feel very unwell, faint or clammy.

Avoid contact sports or very vigorous exercise.

Take care to avoid injury when doing day-to-day things like cooking and gardening.

Feeling sick

Take anti-sickness drugs.

Tell one of your hospital team if they don't work.

Try travel sickness wristbands from the pharmacy. These prevent nausea by using acupressure points.

Try relaxation techniques.

Avoid cooking smells and seek help with preparing meals.

Eat smaller meals that are cold or at room temperature.

Keep your surroundings as peaceful and clean as possible, and try to get some fresh air.

Change in taste and loss of appetite

Try to eat little and often and avoid big meals. Eat whenever you are hungry, whether or not this is your usual mealtime.

Try foods that taste stronger – marinated foods, savoury rather than sweet. Eat food warm rather than hot.

Rinse your mouth before meals and follow any mouth-care regimen you've been given.

Have a ready supply of things that are quick and easy to prepare.

Try to supplement your diet with nutritious drinks, but not at mealtimes. Drinking through a straw may be helpful.

Eat with others in a pleasant environment.

Take exercise where possible.